DOING THE
RIGHT THING
The Ultimate Profit

Robert D. Sherer

A Criterion House Book

DOING THE RIGHT THING

Second Edition, Revised, 1996
Copyright © 1993, 1996 by Robert D. Sherer.
All Rights Reserved

First Edition Printing, 1993
Second Edition Printing, May 1996

ISBN Number: 1-884162-04-5

Published by Criterion House
Oceanside, CA 92058

Distributed by Performance Plus
Westlake Village, CA 91361
1-800-545-3998

Printed in the United States of America

ACKNOWLEDGMENTS

My sincere thanks to the following: Barbara Aiken, Dave Derby, Pat Flood, Leslie Jones, Judy Mantia, Mike Perrault, Harry Ruotsala, Jerry Sullivan, Jim Valestrino, and all of our clients who believe in the people side of quality.

My deep and sincere appreciation and thanks to Phyllis Humphrey for her guidance in the assembly of this work. Her patience and understanding of Sherer-speak made this effort special to me and, I'm sure, to all who read on.

Thanks, also, to our publisher whose sage advice and vision forced me to produce a higher quality product.

This book is dedicated, with deepest gratitude, to my wife Stella, who, through God's hand, has charted our course and helped us to grow and learn the lessons within these pages.

CONTENTS

PREFACE

The crown of all faculties is common sense; it's not enough to know to do the right thing, it must be done at the right time and place. Talent knows what to do... tact knows when and how to do it.

William Matthews

Welcome. You have entered into a world of concepts, ideas and strategies that have been proved to elevate productivity, customer satisfaction and profits. In addition, the companies, teams and organizations profiled within these pages provide a road map to the enhancement of your life and the lives of those around you.

Furthermore, this book is a challenge. I challenge you to put just one or two of the tried and proven ideas in this book into practice in your organization or department. Change is scary and often difficult; but what's impossible is expecting a different result without changing. Even scarier is downsizing an organization, terminating people's careers and upsetting their lives. Yet, too often, downsizing has become the solution of choice—the easy out—rather than taking unfamiliar steps to grow.

Books on business are nothing new. They're gathering dust on the bookshelves of corporate executives everywhere. The credenzas of still other executives are filled with three-ring binders they collected at the seminars they attended while trying to learn how to fix their system, and whose contents were long ago forgotten.

If all we need to know about improvement has already been said, why are businesses continuing to fail at the rate of 15 percent a year? Why do 90 percent of new companies fail? Is it because short-term goals and public relations buzz-words are allowing us to create an *image* of quality, rather than quality itself? Is it fear of change?

Someone once gave me a good definition of insanity: continuing to do the same things and expecting a different outcome. I often ask audiences why they do things the way they do, and the response from the majority is, "That's the way we've always done it." We have become a nation, for the most part, of people who are "ruttized," stuck in a rut of doing things the same old way. Why is change so difficult in a free society? We think about it, we read about it, we talk about it, but we don't *do* it!

Change is not something we come by easily; yet it is apparent that organizations that do not implement change for quality will perish. Just as surely as a limb atrophies from lack of use, so will our minds and our organizations.

Managers have said to me, "I know the diagnosis; where's the prescription? How can we get the people to *want* to change, to improve?" Still others have said, "We *have* made changes—we do it all the time—but where is the improvement, the profit?"

I have the answers to these questions, and they will be presented in words of few syllables so anyone can understand them.

This book is different from others because, during my years in the corporate world—and having founded Quality Concepts, a consultive training company in Westlake Village, California, ten years ago—I discovered many truths, methods, and attitudes that have infused people with the desire and energy to put better ideas into practice. Not just once or twice, but consistently. The bottom-line results in the companies whose stories are profiled in this book confirm these concepts.

Business improvement is not a program. It's a process to be learned and followed, and there are three all-important rules for its success. The process must:

- Involve *everyone* in the organization.
- Be never-ending.
- Be created and implemented in a partnership with outside experts.

High performance is not just sending a bunch of defect-free "blivets" out the back door. It's eliminating poor management practices, short-term profit motives and destructive attitudes on the part of both management and employees. It's creating satisfied customers.

More than that, high performance is a concept of Life, of making continuous improvement in both personal and professional decisions that not only elevate the bottom line, but improve people.

The key question is: Are you P.F. (Performance Fanatic) material? Are you bold enough to take the challenge to change and go out on the end of the limb where the good fruit is? Are you committed to developing a set of core values that quantify profitability, personal growth and the pride of knowing you did the right thing?

Robert D. Sherer, 1996

Doing the Right Thing

DOES IT WORK?

If a man . . .make a better mousetrap . . .you will find a broad, hard-beaten road to his house, though it be in the woods.
Ralph Waldo Emerson

T QM, SPC, TOC. All these acronyms represent quality-speak, the secret language of consultant gurus sweeping across the country to save America from our dreaded offshore competition and mostly from itself. Yes, the organizational development movement has become an industry in itself and, more recently, a fad, one that's constantly reinventing itself, like re-engineering. *Fortune* Magazine reports that many TQM programs are failing, and Tom Peters laments that only one percent of American companies have a true quality process in place.

What's wrong here? We are infused with the short-term, quarter-to-quarter mentality; and if the profits aren't there immediately, or the program takes time, we'll cut corners or back off entirely. I have proof that a quality improvement process (*process*, not *program*) not only will work, it will exceed your wildest expectations in terms of profitability, customer satisfaction and employee loyalty and productivity. And the answer is *so* simple. It doesn't require the tablets from the mountain or an M.I.T. degree. It requires one motivated leader who is a Performance Fanatic, either born or made, to do the right thing right the first time. Maybe you are a latent P.F. I hope so. Here's the first of many examples you will read in these pages of individuals who meet this criteria.

INTERVIEW with HOMEBANC, Atlanta, Georgia

"In 1985 HomeBanc Mortgage Corporation was a relatively unknown lending institution. It had grown as the mortgage arm of Home Federal Savings and Loan Association, an old and established banking institution with roots in Atlanta, Georgia, since 1929. In 1985, that landmark year for the mortgage company, Patrick Flood was hired as a loan officer right out of Winthrop College in North Carolina. Already married and devoted to his wife and the idea of providing a good living for his family, Pat began building his reputation in the banking industry.

"In Pat's first year in mortgage banking he produced more than $25 million in loans, a record-setting production for HomeBanc. Relying on his outstanding leadership ability and entrepreneurial spirit, Mr. Flood established and became manager of the Cobb County, Georgia, Branch of HomeBanc in 1987. Personally selecting and training a handful of energetic and youthful professionals, he guided the branch to the number one retail position in residential lending in the Cobb market.

"According to a former CEO of a Fortune 500 company, 'Your reputation reflects the behavior you exhibit day in and day out through a hundred small things. The way you manage your reputation is by always thinking and trying to do the right thing every day.' This has become Pat's credo for himself and for HomeBanc Mortgage Corporation. Following this path, Pat was promoted to Vice President in 1988 and quickly became recognized as a hands-on manager and motivator focused on providing quality service by a well trained and committed staff.

"Recognizing that the key to success rested in one's ability to effectively communicate and impart knowledge, Pat Flood developed and instituted an employee training program which is recognized as one of the best in the industry. Not coinci-

*dentally, it was in 1988 that HomeBanc began its unprece-
dented growth in revenue production. The company was on
its way to its current reputation for superior service, a passion
for quality and care for its customers.*

*"Pat knew the importance of his associates (Pat insists on
his employees addressing each other as 'associates') and the
community in which he did business. He instituted an
Emergency Fund within his company for associates experiencing unexpected difficulties. He hired a masseuse as part of an
employee stress-reduction program. HomeBanc contributes
regularly to causes such as Habitat for Humanity and numerous women's and children's shelters. He stresses to his
associates the importance of care and attention to one's
family. The result: a value-driven organization that treats each
family member—internally and externally—with mutual respect
and admiration.*

*"While employee turnover is a constant in the banking
industry, HomeBanc is an exception. Only 10 sales people
have left a more than 70 loan officer team in the last five
years. Many associates have been with Pat from the beginning.*

*"After a one-year tenure as Senior Vice President in 1990,
Mr. Flood became Executive Vice President of HomeBanc in
1991. In 1995, the inevitable occurred and Pat was made
President of HomeBanc Mortgage Corporation. He maintained
HomeBanc's image and reputation of fast processing and
quality service. In 1988 HomeBanc produced $130 million.
1996 projections are for over $900 million, with HomeBanc
Mortgage Corporation being Atlanta's leading lender since
1992, a Deerfield Beach, Florida, office placing in the top ten
residential lenders in Broward County, and an Orlando office
which is the fastest growing in Central Florida.*

*"Indeed, Pat and HomeBanc have consistently done the
right thing. Maybe it is because of Pat's ability to visualize
and adapt to changes in the industry; maybe it's his ability to
surround himself with talented and similarly motivated people.
But, regardless, his reputation is that of a motivated, quality
driven and entrepreneurial leader, who genuinely cares and is*

committed to his professional and personal family.   His company mirrors that commitment.   Pat clearly has the ability to see the Golden City over the hill and his proficiency to articulate that vision to his associates is the stuff of which legends are made."

What is the secret of Pat Flood's success?   Pat is a PF, a performance fanatic.   Right from the beginning, he recognized the need to surround himself with winners; and the sales culture, focused on quality and customer service, began to take shape.   His organization was to be based on a value system.   Success would be there for those who operated in a manner consistent with the highest level of morals and values.   Furthermore, it required responding to the customers' needs, delivering outstanding service.   He calls that system his "toolbox," and it contains a deliberate personal improvement plan that includes both training and ethics.

In a speech given to a banking association in March, 1996, Pat said, "I started out in management in 1987 by telling those around me that I wanted to go out to dinner in the community where I lived, and see my customers and not be embarrassed."

Responding to Pat's vision, the sales associates not only focused their attention on establishing themselves as the most dedicated service providers, they also committed themselves to beginning their work day while all of their competitors were still sleeping. Pat began a morning ritual of 7:00 a.m. sales meetings two days a week. If you were late, you were locked out of the office and had to pay a fine of $50. He is constantly on the search for high-performing talent and is unending in his efforts to recruit and retain the best performers.

As the sales force experienced success, Pat recognized that the administrative departments (processing, underwriting, closing) needed to have the same level of intensity and commitment as the sales group. Two years ago, Pat realized the need to bring in a formal quality process to continue the company's growth and contacted Quality Concepts; and this consists of, among other things, custom-built workshops for leadership, associate development, and continuous "doing it right the first time" sessions for all. As a result, the company can underwrite 50 percent of loans in the first 48 hours. The average application to closing is ten days, and they're working toward shortening it to seven days.

The associates at HomeBanc know where they're going. Because of Pat's values and his ability to break down the corporate vision into understandable goals, the associates will follow him during the most difficult of times. Pat's the kind of man who leaves voice mail messages for associates to encourage and recognize specific performance. Interestingly, when associates retrieve their voice mail, they find it was recorded at 3 a.m. or from 35,000 feet, as Pat was winging his way to conduct business in another area. His vision for the future is to build a service delivery system, invest in people and to operate with the highest degree of integrity. And last, but not least, to pray.

Additional interviews, scattered throughout the book, will—I'm certain—convince you that, yes, attention to quality does work, *when it's done right.*

To get where you're going, you need to know where you've been.
Robert D. Sherer

2

WHAT HAPPENED?

Success is simply a matter of luck. Ask any failure.

Earl Wilson

Here we were: the United States, the greatest country in the world built on personal freedom. We invented everything from light bulbs to radios to automobiles, creating wealth, jobs, culture, a beacon for quality in the world. Pride and entrepreneurship abounded. What happened?

HOW DID WE GO WRONG?

I have my own theory, and it's borne out by my experience and almost everything I read and see. Before World War II, the country suffered from a long depression that began with the stock market crash of 1929 and worsened because of a seven-year drought that devastated crops and turned much of the central United States into a dry, wind-blown dust bowl.

I've always felt that people who lived through the depression were blessed with a very special advantage over those of us who came along later. I've come to term that "The Depression Syndrome." People who lived through that era either experienced a lack of—or were in close proximity to others without—enough food to eat or warm clothing to wear. Seeing this kind of misery first hand gave them a deep appreciation not only for a job, but for the basic necessities of life.

In the recession of the '80's and early '90's, unemployment rose to 10 percent and was considered drastic and untenable. But during the depression of the thirties, unemployment reached 25 percent! And in those days there was no unemployment insurance, no Social Security, no aid to dependent children, few welfare programs of any kind.

The great American poet and philosopher, Carl Sandburg, once said that the three things people need to exist are enough food to eat, a warm dry place to sleep, and freedom. We can only appreciate Sandburg's comments when we observe on a first hand basis those who don't have these necessities of life. We continue to watch the horrors of starving African families and it touches us deeply. However, television satellite pictures don't bring the message home quite as clearly as seeing your own family or neighbors standing in the bread line or begging on the corner.

Someone once told me that, when a child, he saw his father take off his overcoat and give it to neighbor man in the street who had lost everything. He said that until that day—in my workshop—he hadn't understood the full impact of the incident. It made him feel very fortunate because he realized they had enough to eat and a coat to give to someone else.

Why should living through that be a blessing? Because people who have a respect for work—knowing that without a job they can't have food, clothing and shelter—have a greater desire to bring craftsmanship to it, and a caring attitude that is often absent in work places today. And I think they were happier.

We hadn't entirely climbed out of that depression when, with the bombing of Pearl Harbor in 1941, we entered a world war. The work place changed. Women entered the work force as never before, as riveters, welders and other factory workers. Men or women, those workers brought with them a concern and care that resulted in a very high quality of work. It's easy to do quality work when you understand the importance of the product you're building; when it may help save a life, possibly that of your own loved one far away at the front, fighting for a freedom that few countries in this world enjoy. The level of quality that this kind of work evokes can't be measured. It comes from the burning desire to do the very best job, because there may never be an opportunity to do it over again.

In spite of all our efforts, however, thirty million people died in World War II. When it was finally over, and peace had come at last; when factories could turn from making bombs to making consumer goods, we all went a little bit crazy. It was time to party! We didn't have to save string anymore. We didn't have to save tinfoil or cooking fat. (Yes, people really did save those things!) Now we could even throw things away!

We wanted everything we'd been denied for so long. This country had such a pent-up buying demand that we would buy anything. We gobbled up products as fast as they could be made. For the first time in our society, people bought things that had absolutely no redeeming features. Look at the Pet Rock. Look at the hula hoop. It was one of the first grown-up toys. Everybody had to have one. And people began to keep up with the Joneses. We had to have *things*. We used to love people and use things. Now, many times, we love things and we use people.

And we wanted these things now! Instant gratification was to become a way of life in the U.S. Whatever we bought had to be bigger and flashier than before. Remember the tailfins on automobiles? And it had to get to us faster. We weren't willing to wait. When the salesperson said it would be ready next Tuesday, we responded with, "If I wanted it Tuesday, I'd be here Tuesday. I want it now!" So we began to put up with some shoddy workmanship. The concern for quality was overridden by impatience.

Let's go back again for a moment to what things were like before World War II. We were craftspeople. Workers served an apprenticeship until the skill level achieved was satisfactory to guarantee the quality of the product. The potter had to mix the mud, sit at the feet of the "master" for a sufficient period of time. The printer's "devil," after years of apprenticeship, often knew more about the press than the "old man." Aspiring managers served as assistants and learned what management was about; they paid their dues. They were dedicated to learning, to bettering their place in the company or community. Only the serious and hardworking survived.

Those were the days of the slogan, "The customer is always right." During the Great Depression, some men sold apples and shoelaces on street corners. They stood in line to get free soup and bread. They weren't customers because they had no money to buy anything. If you had a job in those days, before you went home you stuck your head in the boss's door and said, "Is there anything else you want me to do before I leave?" And you were thinking, "I'll show up early tomorrow morning too, because *I want this job!*" Today, often a job has become a random incident in the lives of people with no desire or direction, who only "suit up, show up and screw up"!

As long-ago shopkeepers or manufacturers, when we found a customer with money to spend, we treated him[1] like royalty. Nothing was too good for him, because he might buy something and keep *us* from having to sell apples on street corners.

But after the war, there were more customers than products. Most of the men were home again; and many of the women, who had worked outside the home for the first time because of the war effort, kept right on working and earning money. Everything was old and worn out and had to be replaced. Factories hummed with machines turning out the products that everyone wanted. Customers began to lose their status. Shopkeepers could tell them, "If I don't sell it to you, Mister, I can sell it to someone else. Get in line. Do you want it or not?"

This scenario played out for a long time. We started out being the best and we knew it. We had the highest standard of living,

---

[1]Throughout this text, I may use the male pronoun for simplicity, but be well assured I mean either sex.

the most of everything. And then, somewhere along the way, we began to change. We had no competition, so we became complacent. Employees worked slower and with less attention to detail; they became more concerned with their wages, their hours and their benefit package, than with the quality of the product they produced; and their unions protected their jobs. Management also succumbed to a short-term philosophy. Everybody wanted an office, a secretary and the key to the executive washroom. Now.

Meanwhile, over in Japan and what became West Germany—defeated countries—things were different. They were desperate. They knew they had to work hard to rebuild and they were willing to try anything to survive. They learned that the only way to compete in world markets was to utilize their work ethic and make superior quality products like the U.S. once made.

When I was a child, playing in the backyard of my home in suburban Washington, D.C., like most little boys, I liked toy cars and trucks. I soon discovered that the ones that fell apart and broke quickly usually said, "Made in Japan" on the bottom. That label meant cheap and shoddy to us. We didn't want those toys; we wanted toys made in America. "Made in the U.S.A." was a guarantee of quality. The Japanese of those days knew that too, and, since there was a town in Japan with the name of Usa, they began to stamp "Made in Usa" on the bottom of their inferior products to confuse us into buying them. But you can't fool a kid or a customer for long.

Today "Made in Japan" usually means quality; and it's more likely the American toy that's cheap and shoddy. How did that happen? To begin with, let's look at the Toyoda family which manufactured textile machinery in the late 19th century. According to *The Machine that Changed the World,* a five-year study from M.I.T., published in 1991 by Harper, Perennial, Kiichiro Toyoda visited the Ford Rouge plant in Detroit in 1929 and realized that automobile manufacturing would be "the industry of industries." In 1937, his nephew, Eiji Toyoda, formed the Toyota Motor

Company, changing the name because Toyoda means "abundant rice field" in Japanese, not an appropriate name for automobiles.

During World War II, the company was forced to build military hardware and trucks; but after the war, they once again began to make automobiles. Toyoda understood it would be imperative to export their products—because very few people in Japan at that time could afford to buy an automobile—and decided to build a defect-free economical vehicle that would appeal to the entry level user.

For many years Toyota's workforce was composed largely of former agricultural workers, and the firm was often viewed as a bunch of farmers; but their strategy of building better and better automobiles resulted ultimately in the Lexus, with a ready-made market of people who began driving Toyotas in the '60's. Once, General Motors, Ford and Chrysler were the hallmarks of automotive excellence. Today, Toyota is recognized as the highest quality producer of motor vehicles in the world.

The joke I often tell to audiences when I start a talk is about three businessmen who were taken hostage in Beirut: a Frenchman, a Japanese and an American. The captors met with the three hostages and indicated they were going to kill them, but first they would grant each of them one last wish. The Frenchman said, "I would like to have a bottle of Lafitte Rothschild '55." They produced it, he drank it, then they blindfolded him and shot him. Next the Japanese businessman was asked for his last wish. He said, "I would like to present one more talk on the effectiveness of Japanese quality in the American marketplace." Whereupon the American leaped up and said, "Shoot me now!"

We may be sick and tired of Japanese stories, but do we take note of the fact that *they* don't tolerate defects? Why not? Because, woven into the fabric of Japanese culture is the philosophy that to be disrespectful or cheat is to lose face. Having a reputation for shipping defective products would smear one's family name. We, on the other hand, have come to accept that 10 percent (or more!) of the things we purchase from American companies will be defective.

Not surprisingly, American companies found it both practical and necessary to import products from other countries, because they worked, because they were delivered in a timely fashion, and they cost less. Soon more and more American businesses made the decision to go abroad to have their products made because they could be manufactured at a lower price than by the American work force.

You know this is true. You have only to look at your clothing, your television set, your stereo. Why do the Japanese own Rockefeller Center and 30 percent of the other buildings in New York City? Because we sent them the money to do it by buying their superior products. Some people may not even be aware that American companies once made these same things and they were the best in the world.

This is grossly simplified, of course, and there are American companies which have been in business for generations and still produce quality products in a timely fashion and at a reasonable price. But the pattern of American business practice that was established in the '50's and escalated in the '60's and '70's has now reached such proportions that everyone is aware of it and trying to turn things around. Yet, even today, businesses are still moving to Mexico or other countries to find people who will care enough to do it right the first time for less money. Later in this book you'll read of more companies like Capital Bank of Miami which have found the way to produce high quality products and services, in America, and offer them at a competitive price.

A CASE HISTORY

My own practical experience with a company that started out doing the right thing, but began to do it wrong, was instrumental in my learning the value of quality for success.

I went to work for A-M International as a serviceman. There was a good training program in effect and we were taught to "do it right the first time." This policy was the result of craftsmanship and care for quality that once permeated American workers and provided a sense of pride. And it worked; the company prospered. At its peak it was a highly-placed Fortune 500 company with over 8000 employees worldwide and did over a billion dollars worth of business annually. The employees felt loyal to the company, and fought fiercely to beat any competition.

That was before the days when job-hopping was considered the road to the top. Writing in *Playboy Magazine* in 1966, J. Paul Getty said that if you stay with a company over five years, you're not going to make it to the top; and in those days that was where we all wanted to be.

It was also before the days of Boesky, Milken and Keating, corporate raiders, and leveraged buyouts.

Over the 25 years I stayed with that company, I moved from mechanic to salesman, then to zone manager, branch manager, district sales manager, regional sales manager and finally vice president in charge of 800 sales representatives. But, by the beginning of the '80's, the company was no longer the same. The Japanese were beating us with improved products and competitive pricing. The company was taken over by a corporate raider. Their plan for becoming "lean and mean" was to get rid of older workers whose salaries and benefits were thought to be a drain on profits. I spent three weeks of every month, for months on end, flying across the country, closing facilities and firing people who had worked for A-M for 25 or 30 years. Families suffered and I suffered with every one of them. After eight corporate promotions (read relocations), I was also sick of the constant moving around the country and having to uproot my family.

And employees weren't the only ones suffering. Customers were affected by the deterioration. The company shipped machines with parts missing and lied to customers about when they would arrive. I sat in on meetings at which decisions were made that made no sense whatever from a customer relations standpoint. When I asked, "But what about the customers?" I was told, "To hell with the customers; what matters is the quarterly figures." Slowly but surely, these practices led to even greater loss of revenue; and what had once been a premier company went on the rocks and eventually filed for Chapter 11 bankruptcy. Although out of Chapter 11 today, A-M is a faint shadow of its former self.

I was disillusioned long before then. In 1981, I couldn't take it anymore and asked for a demotion to West Coast District Manager so I could move back to California, where I intended to stay. Two years later I resigned and went to work for Compugraphics as West Coast regional sales manager. It appeared ideal because, in addition to sales management duties, I was to head up the Quality Improvement Team.

It seemed old-fashioned to others at the time, but I felt that American companies were ignoring the lessons of the past, forgetting that hard work, attention to detail, mutual respect between owners and workers, and quality products were the keys to long-term profits. I developed a quality workshop and tried it out in my region. It was so successful that two vice presidents wanted me to meet with the president to discuss instituting the program in the rest of the company. I flew to Boston, but, in spite of my having an appointment, the president was too busy to see me. After waiting in the lobby for two days, I flew back to California.

A few weeks later, another appointment was arranged; again it was canceled. This time, I spent my days jogging around the city, waiting to be called. But the president was too busy to learn what had improved part of the company. He was so immersed in solving problems that he couldn't trouble himself to learn how to prevent them.

Three days later I went home again, and ended up in bed with a herniated disc from too much jogging! The doctor gave me a choice of surgery or weeks in bed. Being a devout coward when it comes to surgery, I elected bed. Those weeks flat on my back gave me plenty of time to think. I resigned from the company by telephone from my bed and tried to figure out a way to get the quality message across to somebody, somewhere, somehow.

I resolved I was never going to "do it wrong" again or hang out with people who did; or if I did, I'd sure as hell know why and learn from it. It was during this time I experienced my epiphany. The flaming sword touched me and I filled pages and pages with quality issues and crafted the original purposes, company name and basic workshop material. Quality Concepts was born to teach the "people side" of quality.

LESSONS FROM A CORPORATE VETERAN

3

Gross ignorance: 144 times worse than ordinary ignorance.

Bennett Cerf

I f there's one thing I've learned from my many years in the business world it's that it's not what's written on your sheepskin that counts, but what's in your guts. I've met many a man and woman without degrees who, using nothing but common sense and a strong work ethic, rose to the top of major corporations. Richard Branson, a high school dropout, who started Virgin Air Lines, comes to mind, among others. On the other hand, I've met MBA's, and others with half the rest of the alphabet behind their names, who have no practical business sense at all. They couldn't hold a conversation with a customer and, in response to the question, "What will the customer think?", have answered, "I don't care what they think."

Have they forgotten, or did they never learn, that in business, whether you're manufacturing a product or providing a service, *The customer pays the bills!*

After World War II, the G.I. Bill assured college opportunities for all veterans; and many, with the help of their degrees, soon attained levels of management that assured them a frustrated and unhappy career. Corporations created the philosophy that an advanced degree was necessary to succeed. Believing this myth, they passed over non-degreed talent, and erected barriers created by untested degrees, while overlooking strength and experience at all levels. It was no longer necessary to serve an apprenticeship, or to work your way up. With enough degrees, you could start well up the management ladder with little, if any, successful work history. What was needed was *Life 101*, or as Rogers and McWilliams put it, "What we wish we had learned about life in school, but didn't."

At 21, with four years in the U.S. Marine Corps behind me (and having achieved the rank of Sergeant twice), I returned home to College Park, home of the University of Maryland. It would have been easy to enter the university; and, as my mother was secretary to the president, it would have been economically feasible. However, I couldn't wait to see what the world had in store for me in the work place.

First I delivered milk, later became a wholesale route driver for the dairy. Knowing nothing of competition or the need to sell products, I simply delivered what was asked for. Several jobs later, I was tending bar at the local University of Maryland college crowd watering hole, simply answering requests of the patrons. After a couple of years of trying to drink as much as was purchased, it began to dawn on me that there was no chance to own the bar or in any way move ahead of what was a stagnating lifestyle. But I didn't know what to do about it.

Just about the time I made this discovery, two fellows I had known vaguely from high school came into the bar. They were on a boy's night out as both were married and somewhat settled down. Compared to my existence, they were steady as a rock! They showed surprise at finding me behind the bar and kiddingly commented on my career achievement to date. Then they proceeded to tell of their jobs with a major corporation. A-M was the IBM of the business machine world at that time. A-M had, in 1932, brought the printed word closer to more people by introducing the small offset duplicator, which ended the days of the ditto and eventually the mimeograph. The addressing machine was a precursor to the computer.

Fortunately, I was in the right frame of mind, at that moment, and became interested in what these fellows told me about how the A-M machines were selling like hot cakes and how their jobs were to install 'em, maintain 'em, and repair 'em in the event of a breakdown.

They gave me the name of their boss and the following day I called and arranged to meet the service manager. I had little knowledge of how a proper interview at a big company was handled, so with much nervousness, I went into downtown Washington, D.C. to meet him. We hit it off from the start. He tested me in electronics, and thanks to some hydraulic and electronic training in the Marine Corps, I passed. Then, for my first experience in the big world of business, we "did lunch."

I was to spend the next 25 years of my life, to the day, with A-M. My wife and daughters lived and breathed it. I had the logo tattooed on my chest, as the saying goes. We became true corporate gypsies, for as the axiom went in those days, "if you don't go, you don't grow." We went. After schooling in maintenance and repair of the machines at corporate headquarters in Cleveland, and two years in the field, we were offered an opportunity to move to San Francisco.

Here my wife and two-year-old daughter Debbie moved into a whole new world; there were no family or friends near by. Yet, when I crossed the California border, I felt I was in the right place for the first time in my life. As soon as I entered the corporate world, a sense of direction hit me. That direction was up. As a service representative, I couldn't wait to be promoted to senior service representative, and then raced for the next move up. Then one day it occurred to me that selling service maintenance agreements was as easy as falling off a log, and without realizing it, I had actually been selling machines and equipment for the sales representatives. The customers believed what I told them; that our presses were the greatest made, they lasted longer, worked better than our competitors'. They believed what I said because I came back again and again and built trust, something all employers, employees and customers long for.

I tried to persuade management to give me a chance in sales, but it took two years, during which I sold repeatedly for the boss's house accounts. That meant he got the commission, but paid none to me because I wasn't really a salesman, but a service technician. It would be easy to look back and resent this man, but I don't. It was a lesson that showed me the kind of person I didn't want to be. But, get a sales territory I did, and without the necessity of spending the time in sales school back in Cleveland, because I was already successful at selling. I learned on the streets and from the customers and competitors. What an education! A practical one is often the best kind. There was a small tattered sign in the proposal department that I will never forget: "Selling is like shaving: if you don't do it every day, you're a bum!"

The real lessons came from writing financial justification proposals for every imaginable business, where I had to learn about the inner workings of the company to whom I wanted to sell. What departments generated what forms, such as advertising and graphics materials? What did they do, why did they do it, and how did it affect other departments and ultimately tie in with cards, envelopes, forms, stationery, purchasing systems, engineering change notices? This was my education. I learned that every business, from the Muni Rail and cable cars to San Quentin, every ship that anchored at Hunters Point in the San Francisco Naval Shipyard, every law firm, every bank, oil company, department store—everything—ran on the paper path. I sold special paper and ink for the condemned (and later executed) Caryl Chessman to write his book (your tax dollars at work). Hospitals and the Stanford Research Center all relied on their duplicating facility, as did the University of California at Berkeley and Davis and state colleges. I was fortunate to help develop, with Bank of America, the magnetic printing that sped bank transactions and check processing, and still does.

The lesson I learned from all of this rich experience and the many business relationships was the truth of the old adage, "Nothing happens until somebody sells something." Somebody has to buy your stuff! When the annual contest came around, my name was at or near the top for five years as the leading salesman worldwide for this multi-national company, because I was building bridges of trust and reliability by learning *the customers'* business needs.

A-M had a traditional "Hundred Club" which one joined by achieving an assigned quota of sales. One year, at an annual Hundred Club meeting for sales leaders, I was introduced to a man who was to have a positive effect on my career. The man's name was Larry Wilson, and he went on to build the successful Wilson Learning Company in Minneapolis. At his session, Larry spoke of "value added," a phrase I was not familiar with, but which made much sense to me, because it meant finding other ways to be of service to a client. I was hungry, a thief, as it were; if I heard a good idea, or could use a strategy for the benefit of my customers and my commissions, I used it. Why not add value to my deal, find out what the clients wanted and then exceed it? Did it work? Yes. Many times customers would call and ask if I could tell them where to buy other items they needed for their company, because they knew of my desire to add value to our transactions. "Value added" cements relationships. If you don't believe it, take a look at some history.

Sears Roebuck made a name by guaranteeing no-hassle returns. Sure it cost them money—sometimes they'd get ripped off—but it put them on the map in retail sales early in the century. Others were afraid of being burned, would not offer "value added" and stayed mediocre or failed. *Craftsman* tools were an example. No matter what you said on returning the product: "I broke it," "It was an accident," "an act of God," it didn't matter. The response was always, "No problem; it's a *Craftsman*." You trusted them; they created a relationship with you. And in fact, you'd pay more for the product because of the relationship.

A busy career woman bought a Sears kitchen range some years ago. It was labeled their "Best" quality and she expected it to be worry and hassle-free. Unfortunately, there were engineering flaws in the design. The woman spent many hours every Sunday just trying to clean it. Finally, nine months later, she wrote to the company and told them what she considered its faults, not asking for a refund, but suggesting they have their engineering department correct the design. A week later she had a letter acknowledging her complaint and the assurance something would be done. Within the month she had a call from the local Sears store asking when they could pick up the stove and give her a complete refund. Sure, they lost money on that particular deal; but how many other products do you suppose she purchased at Sears? And how many times do you suppose the woman told her friends about their response, thus enhancing Sears' reputation?

Look at Nordstrom. I know you're tired of hearing Nordstrom stories; so are their competitors. A workshop attendee told us she thought Nordstrom prices were too high, but went into the store with a friend one day, noticed shoes were on sale and chose two pairs. The first thing that impressed her was that she didn't have to go up to the counter and stand in line while they rang up her sale; she sat on a comfortable chair and the sales clerk (excuse me, they don't call them sales clerks at Nordstrom's: they're associates) did it for her, brought over the charge slip for her to sign and then handed her the wrapped package. Unfortunately, there was a slip-up and she found on returning home that she had two pairs of shoes belonging to someone else. She phoned the store and within the hour the associate arrived at her home to pick up the wrong shoes. Next the correct shoes were hand-delivered, and then a large bouquet of flowers and a note of apology was delivered to her home. Finally, she received another letter of apology together with a gift certificate in the amount of her purchase!

On the other hand, how many times have you had to wait at the counter, money and purchase in hand, while the sales people chatted with one another, or punched a zillion numbers into their cash registers or computers for purposes of inventory control, or picked up a ringing telephone? (In London I learned that clerks don't answer telephones if a customer is at the desk; the person who has taken the trouble to come to the store gets first priority.)

The customer of a variety store had this story to tell. "There were two check-out lanes, but one was closed; and at the other, two store clerks were having a discussion with a woman who wanted to return something. The transaction seemed to take forever, but I waited patiently. When the customer finally left the store, I moved forward, placed my purchases on the counter and waited again. The clerk never looked up at me, but continued writing down something on a form. I finally said, 'Excuse me, but would you please wait on me? I've been here a long time.' Now she looked up briefly, said, 'I'm sorry; you'll just have to wait,' and went back to writing. Totally frustrated, I did something I had never done before: I said, 'No, I don't. I can shop somewhere else.' and I walked out."

Would it surprise you to learn that that store—part of a large chain, by the way—soon closed down for lack of business?

Value Added should be everywhere. Where and when did we start to treat customers so badly that they now expect poor service? Paul Hawkins Company in the San Francisco bay area, sells *Bulldog* garden tools and guarantees your satisfaction *forever*. They want you to be happy with the product for the rest of your life, wouldn't have it any other way.

In time, I was promoted to Assistant Branch Manager in San Jose. The entire family had to make changes, because my income fell by two-thirds when I entered management. But my lovely wife, Stella, the world's greatest, used her skills to stretch a dollar while I made this important change. Some people outside the corporation didn't understand that process, my need to sacrifice in order to learn and gain experience; but I knew that I needed to work my way up again in the area of leading people.

In San Jose I met and worked for a man named Bruce Schroeder. I'd had the experience of working for a boss who taught me what I didn't want to be; Bruce was the kind of person I did want to be. Bruce taught me to treat people with sincere respect and dignity. No matter how hard I had to look, I could find something in all people that was at least redeemable.

The people who worked with Bruce Schroeder never questioned their commission statements or his position regarding fair treatment. Needless to say, they worked hard for him. He shared his vision for branch operations with everyone, from me, the assistant manager, down through the staff, sales, service, stock room, right out to the shipping dock. We all knew where we were going and that if we made our annual numbers, everyone would win. I remember, shortly after arriving for my new assignment, asking Schroeder if we should share some information that came from the home office. Past experience had taught me that bosses often withheld information; in such situations, I felt we never really knew the big picture of the branch and where we were headed. It was everyone for himself. In fact, on occasion, we were pitted against each other, not with the result of strengthening the whole, but driving wedges between departments and individuals. This created mistrust and promoted tactics that furthered individual goals at the expense of others or of the department.

Mr. Schroeder looked at me as if I had just asked a really stupid question; then he said, "Who's going to do the work and carry our team over the goal? All of us! So shouldn't all of us know as much as I do? Our employees are as smart or smarter than we are; why would we keep information from them?"

As a leader, Bruce Schroeder got the thrill of sharing good news, and as a leader, he had the responsibility to keep every person aware when there was bad news. He told me that some people used "Mushroom management: keep 'em in the dark and feed 'em manure," and he thought that was dumb, and people who used it just didn't know any better. Schroeder won company awards every year, but he took none of the credit. He taught me what I've named "mirror management." Whenever he was brought up front to accept an award, he refused the praise for himself and passed it on to his team. But, on the other hand, if we screwed up, the reflection shone on us then too; and we tried to figure out how to fix it or keep it from happening again. It was great to learn from a real pro like Bruce.

Then I was promoted to Los Angeles to take over another larger branch. I was to fix a rundown, broken operation where the employees hadn't worked effectively individually, much less as a team. The previous management of that branch had left its legacy of example: those who goof off and cheat, prosper. By now I'd learned there were two kinds of attitudes about new management coming in to fix things. First there were the people who would either test you in some way, or ignore you and hope you'd go away. The others were lined up outside the door to "suck up" and tell you how happy they are that *you* are the new manager.

Management changes come about for several reasons. Perhaps the company's been sold, or someone dies and must be replaced, or the manager moves up and leaves a winning team behind. However, if you're a strong manager and a fixer, you don't normally inherit a winner and take over a team with a record of winning seasons. No, I got stuff that was broken, rotten or dead and was told to breathe life into it. Actually, that's the way I preferred it! Once, in a conversation about a possible promotion, a national sales manager told me that the branch in question was doing great. I could maybe notch it up a percent or two and no one would notice; but if it slipped one or two percent—if I screwed up—I'd have much to answer for. So the broken-down branch was the one I wanted. Give me your worst and we'll put together some pride and team spirit and take it to the moon. That's fun!

In Los Angeles I inherited a group, some of whom I'd met and partied with in my earlier years with the company, who delighted in the prospect of watching Sherer flounder and sink his first time out as a branch manager. It was then I discovered a strategy that worked for me, and many a manager I trained over the years. Once you've arrived and the welcoming committee has ensconced you in your office with the appropriate amount of pomp and circumstance, they pray you stay in there and that nothing will change. It should come as no surprise to you that human beings hate change and will fight it with unbelievable zeal and resources.

It often happens that, after a new manager arrives, after the hubbub dies down and it's business as usual, he'll discover that the reason he's there—to get things turned around—isn't happening. That's when, as new manager, he stews and frets and finally takes some action. But it's too late; he's old news by now. He can't change people easily, because he, himself, has become a known entity.

In Los Angeles, I knew I had only a short time to get these folks' attention and let them know that a new commander was in charge. From the first minute I arrived, not three days later, or even by lunch. I learned to arrive in the office *very* early in the morning or on a Sunday by way of a key sent in advance of my arrival. By the time the employees arrived for work on Monday, I was at the door to greet *them* to *our* new branch. I had painted my office, hung up my plaques, set out my pictures of my wife and daughters. Sometimes the paint wasn't dry by eight a.m., but by God they knew it was *my* office, and the old guard was gone and forgotten. In one branch we were subsequently sent to, which was in poor condition, I painted all day Saturday and Sunday: not only the office, but also the bathrooms and the lunchroom, and on Monday evening we all got together and painted the large equipment demonstration room.

Those who were interested were among the painting crew, which gave me a fix on some folks immediately. Poor performers were given a set of "to do" lists, and I explained that if they wanted to work for me, this was required. If they didn't do them, they were telling me they no longer cared to work there. I found in one case a fellow who was selling cars at a used car lot during the afternoons instead of working his sales territory. Another was selling equipment out of the branch and pocketing the dollars. People with this level of audacity will eat you for lunch if they even think they can. You must be tough up front and get people's attention. The workers who are honest and hardworking will cheer.

Once you've established that you can be tough and poor performers will not be tolerated, the bad apples will leave of their own accord or be driven out by their peers. If people know there's steel in you, they'll respect you and not forget it. But I've never seen it go the other way. You can't change from being nice to tough; employees will never buy it. I've had the pleasure of working with many men and women I called friends, and we visited in one another's homes and shared family fun. But we all knew that when there was a job to do and goals to be met, it was my responsibility to see that they did their part. When one wins, we all win. If you've got a new job to do, be tough up front; it builds respect. You can loosen up later.

From Los Angeles, I went to Sacramento to fix yet another problem branch; then to Des Moines, Cleveland, and on to Chicago as Regional Manager with escalating dollar responsibilities. Each city was a new challenge, new friends, new relationships with clients and workers. Most important, new lessons.

I always had the ambition and desire to succeed. Ambition is a funny thing; it can make you or break you. For instance, did

Ivan Boesky, Michael Milken or Charles Keating really feel good about what they were doing? Were they happy making millions at the expense of those who saw their jobs disappear and their lives ruined? They're probably sorry now because they were caught; but what about those who are never caught? There's many a guilty party in the great Savings and Loan Bailout that affects every taxpayer in the country. Do they sleep well at night? Will any of them wonder if it was worth it?

While on a visit to San Quentin, I heard—from a convict—the well-known expression, "What goes around comes around." I believe the decade of the '90's is going to be one of a rebirth of ethics in the work place. The fact that these abuses are written and talked about reveals a growing awareness that fundamental changes must be made if America is to take seriously the enormous problems of society. We've already learned that it's absolutely necessary in the business sector, if we're going to build teams that produce quality products to compete in world markets. Trust begins with truth, and honest behavior will also give a new meaning to life.

4

STAGGERING TOWARD QUALITY

Long range planning does not deal with future decisions, but with the future of present decisions.

Peter Drucker

M any bemoan the continued influx of Japanese cars and other countries' products to the United States, but in fact, I look on it as a blessing. It forced us to take a cold, hard look at ourselves. We needed to be rocked where we live or surely we would have sunk to a low from which it would have been impossible to rebound. Some think we're already there and that we'll soon become a Third World nation paying our workers $5 a day.

H. Ross Perot, head of Perot Systems Corp., speaking to a group of Miami businessmen in April, 1991 (before he became a Presidential candidate), deplored this deterioration and said that our country has "the industrial world's dumbest work force." He charged that we must stop treating students of science and technology as nerds. Tom Peters reminds us that we've spent billions on capital equipment, while, "dumbing down the U.S. work force by investing a mere pittance in education."

In an interview in *Time* Magazine, former Labor Secretary William Brock warned that we must either clean up our act or pay for the consequences in a greatly reduced standard of living for everyone. We had economic growth for seven years, but this increased productivity was generated by buying sophisticated equipment. "The rate of improvement is half of what it was 20 years ago," Brock said. "The only reason family income is up is because we've got two-earner families. Wages in real terms are lower today than in 1973." Today, every country in the world can buy the same idiot-proof machinery. If people in other parts of the world will work for $5 a day with the same equipment, why should anyone hire an American who wants $20 or $25 an hour? American workers must either increase their skills or accept lower wages.

The need to increase the skill of its workers is not lost on some businesses. Unfortunately, there are too few of them. Ninety-five percent of money for training is being spent by only one percent of businesses. Brock says the work-force crisis "pales in comparison with the management crisis." Workers cannot solve these problems. Only management can. The Commission on the Skills of the American Workforce proposed charging a tax on companies that don't train their workers sufficiently to keep up with changing requirements, so that 15 to 30 percent of our young people don't drop by the wayside every year, as they do now.

Our university system is one of the finest, but our elementary and secondary education is below every other industrialized nation. Yet only 30 percent of our population goes to college. What happens to the other 70 percent? Who gives them the skills to be productive and competitive in the world? Japanese students graduating high school have an equivalent of four more years of schooling than U.S. students; they attend six days a week, 240 days a year, to our 180.

Brock states: "We are not putting our resources where the kids are. In the city of New York there are more school administrators than there are in all of France. In the state of New York there are more administrators than there are in all of the European Community, and the E.C. has 12 countries and 320 million people."!

If American schools refuse to spend the bulk of their funds on more teachers instead of administrators, it will fall to business to educate its workers after they graduate. They cannot do quality work without education and training; and no complaining to government, no slogans or even programs will change that overnight. We *can* turn the country around—we can turn our companies around—but a total commitment will be necessary.

Often, even when the problem is recognized, improvement isn't forthcoming. Here are some real-life examples of how we approach issues which need addressing. Only the names have been changed to protect the incompetent.

EXAMPLE: YOU *WILL DO* QUALITY

Mr. Jumpon Bandwagon, Senior Vice President, is really caught up in the quality quest. He's read several articles in trade publications and is convinced that profits will grow and his clients will multiply if only his organization can improve the quality of its products. He gathers his management staff and announces that henceforth everyone must make an effort to eliminate mistakes. *And, he is not kidding*; this is really serious!

Mr. Bandwagon has just committed the first deadly sin in the effort to infuse the quality commitment. Each of his managers receives his remarks in his own unique manner, and each in the context of his own understanding of the language Mr. Bandwagon used. By edict, he pronounced that quality will happen, and yet he offers no plan or direction. Each member of the organization perceives quality in his own terms. As a team they would have as many ideas as there were team members. Imagine a football team with eleven different notions of how to score a touchdown on any given play.

EXAMPLE: YOU GO AND THEN TELL US ABOUT IT

Ms. Lettus Delegate, head of another company, is also intrigued by the possibility of increased profits, customer satisfaction and fewer mistakes. Ms. Delegate calls in her staff to discuss the quality issue; she wants their input on the subject. This is a novel and praiseworthy effort by Ms. Delegate in this day and age. She receives a lot of good ideas from her staff and they settle on an effort that will send the key managers to quality training seminars soon to be presented in a pleasant resort area. Although Ms. Delegate wishes she could go, she is too busy. However, her staffers can go and report what they learn to her and to the rest of the organization. This comes under the well-worn heading of "train the trainer."

Mr. I.M. Chosen goes to the seminar and returns with material that is so hot that it glows in the dark. But when he comes back, there are a dozen phone calls to answer and ten serious problems to handle; so a week goes by and the material on his desk doesn't glow so much anymore. In another week, the glow is completely extinguished and the material goes on top of his credenza. And in another week, it goes *into* the credenza, another three-ring binder never to be seen again.

Or, if it's shared with others at all, it gets diluted as it goes down the line, like the old "telephone" game we all played as children. Not to mention that Mr. Chosen is politically sideways with half or more of the staff.

The Second Deadly Sin in creating quality commitment is the thinking that we can pass along feelings, experiences and knowledge to subordinates, peers or senior managers. I'm reminded of my experiences working with convicts in penal institutions. Peers don't take training well from peers, be they convicts, health-care workers, CPA's or senators. Most feel the investment should have been made in *them; they* should have been the ones chosen to go to the seminars. They weren't; therefore it isn't important enough to listen to those whom they perceive to be less deserving than themselves.

Besides, you cannot convey the experience in all senses to another. Like a woman trying to explain what it's like to be pregnant to someone who's never had that experience. *It loses something in the translation.*

Ms. Delegate practices the philosophy of hiring somebody to get quality through applying money, not attention. By training only a few, or the "key" people, the system fails due to lack of involvement by all the people from top to bottom. Look at Xerox and Federal Express. Their outstanding success is due to two things: everyone goes to the meetings and the directions are written down and shared by all. Everyone in that environment knows what quality means, the cost of implementing quality programs, *and* what results to expect. If they participate, every-one wins; if they don't want to participate, they go away. Prob-lems are solved by people who want success for themselves and their team members. Let's face it: the people are the company, no matter how small or large the organization.

EXAMPLE: LET'S DO QUALITY, AND MOVE ON

Mr. Monte Olympus is really serious about this quality commitment; he has read a book about quality and can see the definite benefit to his organization. Mr. Olympus purchases books for all his employees and orders that they be read and adhered to henceforth. Furthermore, the slacker to this commitment will meet with guaranteed grievous consequences. Mr. Olympus issues this edict every time he gets fired up about some issue, especially if he thinks it means more profits.

By blithely going along, assuming the commitment to quality is alive and well in his company, as are all the missiles of good ideas he has hurled down the mountainside to his workers, Mr. Olympus commits another deadly sin. He manages under the premise that, as he reads and understands, so shall all those on his work roster. When he says it's blue, everyone knows instinctively what color of blue he sees. He becomes engrossed with different trends periodically; and in good conscience, he believes that having initiated major programs, the company will be better and now he can move on to researching the next major policy for the staff to implement.

The problem is, this style of management develops workers who smile without enthusiasm and go about their work knowing that another major program will soon be on its way and—thankfully—that the last one will soon be a brief memory.

EXAMPLE: QUALITY CAN BE FUN

Mr. Jolly Goodtime figures that, with costs going up for personnel, material, et al, it would be timely to reduce costs through reducing errors and at the same time build camaraderie in the organization. Besides, more clients would come to do business with the firm that cares about quality work.

He organizes a Quality Day, invites a famous quality guru to come, and serves lunch in the cafeteria. To top it all off, everyone is given a quality button. The event is a huge success, and for several days everyone talks about the inspirational speaker, how great it was to get together for lunch, and that Mr. Goodtime's comments were really sincere.

Yes, you're right. In 30 days, no one could remember the speaker's name, much less the message. Maybe they could remember what they had for lunch. Maybe.

Mr. Goodtime practices the "let's have a party and create a great affair that will incorporate the message in everyone's mind" method. This can be an excellent first step to infusing the quality message; but not if it is only a one-time effort and doesn't address the long-term commitment necessary to deepen the quality results and the return from the ultimate product. Mr. Goodtime can't understand why employees keep screwing up and customer complaints continue. And after all he spent on that quality extravaganza six months ago!

EXAMPLE: WE WANT QUALITY NOW

Mr. Grimly Impatient is really a serious, dedicated customer-oriented manager, who is very concerned about quality and wants to do something about it. So, after much thinking and consulting with his staff, he decides to retain a quality training company to work with all phases of his organization.

Mr. Impatient always measures things carefully and enjoys the benefit of results. Conversely, he doesn't suffer well the pain of loss. Since he has learned to manage in a "hands on" way, if positive results aren't forthcoming quickly, he cuts his losses. Quickly.

Now Mr. Impatient has the company's attention, and the quality training people are in the trenches with the troops, toiling with the intricacies of understanding job functions and placing devices for management communication. In other words, the battleship is about to alter course when, to the dismay of all, Mr. Impatient, practicing his dominant management style, perceives nothing is happening and results are not commensurate with effort and investment; so, as per his philosophy, he gets rid of a losing proposition.

He practices the start and stop method: "try it and see if it works." This is a short-term approach and it *won't work*. Without the long-term commitment to programs, a yo-yo effect drives the organization up and down and suffers the attendant grief that goes along with such activity. The cost in employee turnover in such companies tends to be very high.

WRONG CHOICES

There were a lot of reasons for the reversal of fortune suffered by A-M International, no longer a formidable presence in the office products industry. Two such reasons involved lost opportunities. A story is told about the A-M President, Basil Ward, who had been given a demonstration of the early version of Remington Rand computer memory capability. Afterward, he said, in effect, "You can store up to six lines of data on an Addressograph plate: why would you want more?"

When John Carlson of Haloid Corp. (the company which became Xerox) was looking for investors, he thought A-M was a perfect match. Imagine a device to make copies from existing originals without redrawing or retyping! The response attributed to Mr. Ward after the presentation was, "Why would anyone want another way to make copies? A secretary can make up to six carbons and after that type an offset master to produce additional copies."

Lack of vision isn't the only management shortcoming these days. During the past two decades managers more often came from the accounting department than the shop floor. Looking *only* for bottom line results can lead to short-term solutions that ultimately leave the company worse off than before. The professional CEO's hired by many companies in the last couple of decades employed just such tactics. They aimed for next-quarter figures that looked better than last; and America as a whole gradually found its machines out-dated, its work force untrained and its market share deteriorating. Not to worry: the professional CEO had his personal parking place, private elevator, and, ultimately, (when the board of directors caught on to his failure) his "golden parachute" that let him walk away with millions.

And the arrogance of much corporate top management is matched or exceeded by the arrogance in Washington. Americans are screaming for changes in government too; yet, in spite of the mismanagement of our entire country, the trillion-dollar debt, the corruption in some welfare programs, educational and health-care systems that are among the worst in the Western world, our legislators bleat pitifully at the thought they should have their terms in office limited. It's time to get rid of some incumbents and let non-millionaires, women and minorities have a crack at solving our problems. But the lawmakers won't go gracefully. *Of course* all those people in Congress want to keep their jobs: jobs where they can determine their own salary and perks (regardless of their poor performance or what their employers—the people—want), establish their own pensions, and set their own rules of conduct. Who wouldn't?

If you don't believe this, think about why millions begged Ross Perot to run for President and the 20 million who voted for him.

THE DEMING PRIZE

Nevertheless, a few people *are* staggering toward quality. Everyone in business today knows the name of W. Edwards Deming. Forty years ago that was not the case. All but ignored by American industry, he went to Japan. It's ironic, isn't it, that an American went to the country we'd just defeated in a terrible war, and laid the groundwork for them learning to beat us at our own game? It wasn't until the '80's that U.S. companies began to pay attention to Deming's principles. He was hired by both Ford and General Motors, and his methods inspired managers at Xerox and IBM. His fourteen points for management were not lost on Federal Express and Florida Power and Light, either.

What are these fourteen points? Although you may have them in a book, a memo, or a plaque on your wall, they bear repeating:

1. Create constancy of purpose toward improvement of product and service to become competitive and to stay in business and to provide jobs.

2. Adopt the new philosophy. We are in a new economic age. Western management must awaken to the challenge, must learn their responsibilities and take on leadership for change.

3. Cease dependence on inspection to achieve quality. Eliminate the need for inspection on a mass basis by building quality into the product in the first place.

4. End the practice of awarding business based on the price tag. Instead, minimize total cost. Move toward a single supplier, for any one item, and establish a long-term relationship of loyalty and trust.

5. Improve constantly and forever the system of production and service to improve quality and productivity, and thus constantly decrease cost.

6. Institute training on the job.

7. Institute leadership. The aim of leadership should be to help people and machines and gadgets to do a better job. Supervision of management is in need of overhaul, as well as supervision of production workers.

8. Drive out fear so that everyone may work effectively for the company.

9. Break down barriers between departments. People in research, design, sales and production must work as a team, to foresee problems of production and in use that may be encountered with the product or service.

10. Eliminate slogans, exhortations and targets for the workforce asking for zero defects and new levels of productivity. Such exhortations only create adversarial relationships, as the bulk of the causes of low quality and low productivity belong to the system and thus lie beyond the power of the workforce.

11a. Eliminate work standards (quotas) on the factory floor. Substitute leadership.

11b. Eliminate management by objective. Eliminate management by numbers, numerical goals. Substitute leadership.

12a. Remove barriers that rob the hourly worker of his right to pride of workmanship. The responsibility of supervisors must be changed from sheer numbers to quality.

12b. Remove barriers that rob people in management and in engineering of their right to pride of workmanship. This means, *inter alia*, abolishment of the annual or merit rating and of management by objective.

13. Institute a vigorous program of education and self-improvement.

14. Put everybody in the company to work to accomplish the transformation. The transformation is everybody's job.

Deming grew up in poverty and developed an appreciation for the needs of the poor and for making a dollar stretch. He abhorred waste. It alarmed him, after World War II, to see American companies forget their heritage of good craftsmanship and reliability and go down the road of expedience. "Quality," he said, "starts at the top." But no one listened. They're beginning to listen now.

As it happens, Japan was the ideal place for Deming's principles to work, because the Japanese already had a national characteristic called *kaizen*. The essence of *kaizen* is improvement, continuous improvement, and this is part of their culture. A gardener, for example, will seek to improve his garden every day, even if all he does is move a rock from one place to another. More so than Americans, Japanese understand that everything changes constantly and, furthermore, that it *must* change.

The Deming Prize, introduced 40 years ago when Deming donated his lecture fees to the Union of Japanese Scientists and Engineers, is the most highly coveted prize in Japan. Winning it is the goal of every Japanese company. Named for an American, it's almost a guarantee of quality. The examination required of competitors includes on-site inspection of plants and facilities, questions of both managers and workers about their goals, their processes, their training, their solution to problems, and their safety record, all of this readily backed up by verifiable facts and figures. It not only influenced Japanese managers, but inspired American companies to compete for the prize and establish something similar in this country.

THE MALCOLM BALDRIGE NATIONAL QUALITY AWARD

Established in 1987, the first awards, named for the former United States Secretary of Commerce, were given by President Ronald Reagan in a White House ceremony in the fall of 1988. Notable winners are:

1988:   Motorola
        Westinghouse (Nuclear Fuel Div.)
        Globe Metallurgical Inc.

1989:   Milliken & Co. (not the junk bond dealer)
        Xerox (Business Products Div.)

1990:   Federal Express (First service company to win)
        Cadillac (First auto company)
        IBM (Its 400 Plant)
        Wallace Company, Houston, TX

1991:   Marlow Industries, Dallas TX
        Solectron Corp, San Jose, CA
        Zytec Corp, Eden Prairie, MN

1992:   AT&T (Network Systems Group, Transmission
              Systems Business Unit)

AT&T (Universal Card Services)
Granite Rock Company
Texas Instruments Inc.,
     (Defense Systems & Electronics Group)
Ritz-Carlton Hotel Company

1993:   Ames Rubber Corp. (Small business)
         Eastman Chemical Company (Manufacturing)

1994:   AT&T Consumer Communications Services
         (Service)
         GTE Directories Corp. (Service)
         Wainwright Industries, Inc. (Small Business)

1995:   Armstrong World Industries, Inc.
             Building Products Operations (Manufacturing)
         Corning, Inc. Telecommunications Products
             Division (Manufacturing)

The program is a joint effort by both government and private enterprise that has already received millions in donations and is run by the U.S. Standards Institute, the American Society for Quality Control and the American Productivity and Quality Center. To apply, companies must document up to 75 pages of efforts to improve quality, and not every company that applies is actually approved for competition. Nevertheless, more and more companies apply for the award every year and are willing to spend as much as twelve months improving their facilities, work standards and procedures to gain the recognition this award offers. Since the judges have no obligation to award any prizes at all in any given year, they can insist on their high standards. Unlike the Oscars, where, in a year of mediocre motion pictures, a film will nevertheless win a statue, the Malcolm Baldrige Award is not a competition among entrants but to a standard that indicates a commitment to the quality so desperately needed if we are to compete in the global market place. Some winners of the award are even insisting their *suppliers* make the same aim for excellence and apply for the prize. If you're interested, you can call 301-975-2036.

THE COMPETITION

Nine of the world's ten largest banks are Japanese. They have fully, or partially, acquired 150 electronics companies and are now moving into the service and entertainment fields.

The Japanese—and all our other competitors, world-wide—have awakened us to our shortcomings. But there's still time to change for the better. We stand on the edge of a magnificent garden to be planted, tended, and harvested again and again. If only leaders—in both corporations and government—are willing to embrace some simple concepts to assure the crops, then everybody from the uppermost management to the smallest customer will enjoy all the benefits that a quality commitment will ensure.

Quality service stories are emerging from all avenues of business as well as in the volunteer sector. Turnarounds of monumental proportions are occurring. When a leader with vision and energy hones in on the quality issue, watch out; the ride can be painful because it requires change, but the results are amazing.

Even as you read this, some managers and employees are sitting in quality workshops with eyes glazed over and are missing this message. Help wake them up! Become a P.F. (Performance Fanatic) if you're not already. If you're reading this, chances are you have a P.F. brand on you someplace, or you'd be watching television to see this year's equivalent of who shot J.R. Performance fanatics lead full, rich, exciting lives through the quest for continuous improvement in their lives and their careers, and they savor fuller, more satisfying days.

5

WHAT IS QUALITY?

Trifles make perfection, and perfection is no trifle.

Michelangelo

"Why is it there's never time to do it right, but there's always time to do it over?"

I found this motto hanging on the wall of a little print shop in Washington, D.C. over 30 years ago, and it's the root of the quality issue. When executives tell us they can't begin the quality process now, guess what excuse they give? They say they don't have *time*!

If you called in ten people from your organization and asked them, "What is Quality?" you'd get ten different answers. Maybe eleven. Actually there are no wrong answers. Many attendees of Quality Concepts workshops indicate that their definition of quality is doing the best job they can, and taking pride in their work.

Management may not always think of quality in terms of "doing my best;" yet if that's the perception of the employees, it's real to them. It just may not be enough to match your customers' expectations.

Webster defines quality as a degree of excellence. I think quality is a process of learning how to provide products or services that someone is willing to pay for, in order to stay in business and make a profit that allows us the kind of food, shelter and freedom that we want.

With fierce competition coming at us from all sides, quality becomes the key word in productivity, and productivity is a ratio between what you put in and what you get out of any process. Quality products and services, at lower cost, add to the bottom line and provide everyone a higher standard of living. There is no other way.

THE HARD HAT MENTALITY

When I first began talking about quality to businesses, I was often told, "That doesn't apply to us. We don't make a hard product; we have no inventory or parts department, no assembly line, no packing and shipping department." Unless they manufactured a blivet, they didn't think they needed to think about quality.

Now, suddenly, it appears American business has become determined to corral and harness the quality service issue. The stream of statistical quality books is endless, ranging from texts used in schools which teach the subject, to self-help and industry manuals and tapes geared to increased productivity. Yet most deal with quality on the shop floor, and not with the equally important issue of quality service.

This blind spot in the perception of quality might be called the "hard hat mentality." It's predicated on the concept that quality refers only to products you can touch or feel; quality of service is seldom given a second thought. Yet responsive service is essential for long-term repeat business and positive word-of-mouth advertising.

Executives with a strong desire to attack poor quality—or simply raise the level of current quality—often believe that remedies are appropriate only for those people in the organization who specifically handle tangible products.

Consider, however, that all products are not necessarily made of assembled pieces. This concept, while sometimes difficult to grasp, is at the heart of the quality issue.

Leaders must eventually realize that the *invoice* for the hard product is just as viable a product as the blivet produced on the assembly line. Even the message taken by the receptionist or secretary is just as valuable a product!

THE REAL ORGANIZATIONAL CHART

Everyone has seen a chart representing the various levels of organization in a company. Ideally they're pyramid shaped and look something like this :

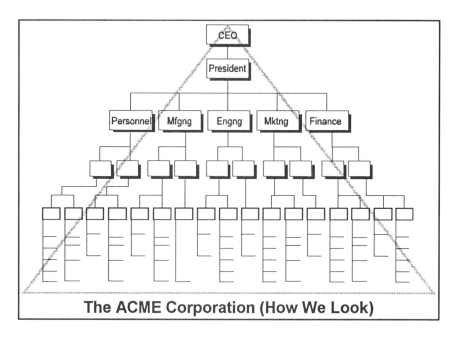

The ACME Corporation (How We Look)

Up at the top is the CEO. Then the President, overseeing everything that goes on, the person with primary operating responsibility. Beneath him or her are various levels of management with different functions. That can be divided still further, and finally you get down to the troops, the people who do the real work. In the interest of space, the chart has been simplified; in most American companies there are so many layers of management between vice presidents and workers that the chart resembles a silo more than a pyramid. Someone recently joked, "They need them; the main duty of managers is to solve problems created by too many managers."

The pyramid is the way it's *supposed* to operate. But in reality, we all know the truth is something like the figure on the next page. Here's the big cheese up at the top. He may be asleep at the switch. You have the real head underneath him, the one other wheels gravitate toward (when they're not squabbling amongst themselves). The star in the upper right, is really just a small wheel who perceives himself to be CEO material. But his rocket has singed a few others on the way up and is careening off course. Meanwhile, middle management is occupied with love interests, booze, lunches and most everything else except company business. The staff doses or watches the clock. One frustrated individual tries an end-run around his superiors to no avail. And the phones go unanswered as customers fight a losing battle to get service.

No matter how detailed your organizational chart, the output from *every* box, from the Head Shed to the mail room and loading dock, should be thought of as a product subject to the quality concepts discussed at the beginning of this chapter.

It's essential that management adopt this philosophy in order for it to be accepted and acted on by workers at every level. The administrative sector must focus on the quality of every employee's output or "product," and acknowledge the value and importance of each individual's measurable contribution to the quality strategy. A lack of focus on this issue can sink the organization, or at least assure its mediocrity.

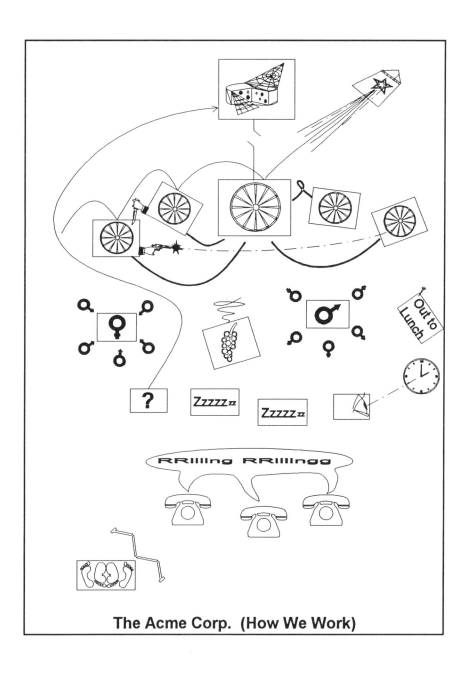

The Acme Corp. (How We Work)

In the '90's, an increasing number of tasks are being relegated to computers and robots, multiplying the demand for service-oriented employees. This trend increases the visibility and responsibility of service personnel, both to customers *of* the business and customers *within* the business.

Who will ingrain in this work force the absolute necessity to provide superior service?   Who will explain that advertising dollars to lure new customers and clients are wasted without genuine concern and attention to every customer's needs and desires? Professional corporations with soft products, as well as those in service-oriented sectors, tend to dismiss the quality issue as irrelevant to their business, except possibly for some customer service smile training.   ("Smile" is also known as "carwash" training: i.e. "run 'em through it.") The employees then interpret this cavalier attitude as company policy, and demonstrate it through half-hearted efforts, such as the cliché, "Have a nice day," and a pass-the-buck attitude.

To elevate the service product in the white collar business area, it's imperative to realize that *all* employees are producing products that must be done right the first time, or someone must

Do it over again!

or say goodbye to more customers.

ELEMENTS OF QUALITY

For an organization to continue operating, more than a feeling of "I did the best I could," is required. To stay in business, you have to satisfy your customers. In fact, the Ritz-Carlton's desire is to anticipate and exceed their guests' requirements. To satisfy them, you have to know what they require, and to find out what they require you have to communicate effectively. Therefore, we can say that three important ingredients of quality are:

- Strong communication
- Understood requirements
- Customer satisfaction

These points will be taken up in detail in other chapters, but for the moment consider them in terms of who does the communicating, learns the requirements and then executes the order to the customer's satisfaction. A recent study reported in the *Wall Street Journal* indicates the average service-based company spends thousands of dollars training managers and executives, yet virtually nothing training other employees. The importance of each individual role must be recognized to instill a sense of purpose and belonging that leads to quality work.

If we want to influence the culture of the organization, it becomes crystal clear that every employee must hear and experience the same message and logic. In this way, all workers come to value their own individual performances, and understand who their personal customers are: that is, the people who are the recipient of their work.

Whether it's the bank teller, the claims clerk, the secretary, the escrow officer, or the surgeon, all have customers inside the organization. It's incumbent, therefore, on management to teach this method of customer-to-customer passage of work to achieve quality of a substantial, long-lasting, cost-effective nature.

Quality will not be achieved immediately; there is no "quick fix" for some problems. They didn't develop overnight and they won't go away overnight. It takes time for the process to show results. Breaking down major goals into several smaller shorter-term goals, such as To-Do Lists, is more effective than trying to make giant steps toward quality. If objectives are too high, the employees may become frustrated and lose enthusiasm.

People become discouraged if their results aren't recognized. Managers should regularly communicate appreciation for efforts to improve quality, and reinforce it at every step. Imagine the cast of a play with no audience reaction or players in sports with no system of score keeping. How would they know if they're winning or losing?

Some executives may reel under the notion of undertaking changes which will require long hours of commitment and many dollars for training. Yet, in the '90's, companies which do not commit to organizational development based on quality service are in for difficult times ahead. (Read: they haven't gone belly-up yet.)

COST OF QUALITY

It's even more surprising, and alarming, to talk with business people who indicate their firm's profitability is assured because the cost is passed along to the client! In some cases, they have the preposterous attitude that the more it costs, the more their customer will value it. The Yuppie is dead and the remaining market niche for the overpriced caviar set is slim.

That attitude isn't what made Ford and General Electric and many of the early giants of industry successful. They offered a quality product that was affordable to every working individual, and their growth and success were guaranteed.

When people are able to buy quality products that cost less and work properly—as they do from many foreign companies—American business must face the fact that some costs cannot be passed along to the client, and that poor quality is very costly indeed!

A recent article in *Fortune* Magazine stated that there are 100 million people employed in the United States. If each one made a simple $10 error each day, the cost would average one billion dollars a day, or up to $365 billion a year. That might surprise you until you explore the real cost of mistakes in business. Recently, one of my clients, a commercial bank, told me that producing a set of loan documents can take up to six hours. If those documents need to be reworked, because of an error, the loan origination fee is *gone*, swallowed up in the pit of hidden costs.

Examples are everywhere, from messages with wrong numbers, to inserting incorrect figures on statements, to sending documents out the door to the wrong party. These occurrences are recorded daily in the best of companies, and are certainly plentiful in the average ones.

It's estimated that business spends an average of $1,200 a year on manager training, but only $1.87 on other employees. Do you have any employees who could cost you $100 if they made a mistake? Or, a better question might be: Who in your hire *couldn't* make a $100 error? Nobody. Then isn't it worth something to train them to do their tasks properly and to look for—and correct—any mistakes?

I'm reminded of a true story that emerged from a manufacturing facility in Chicago, which made a machine that printed paper forms. Several clients complained that the forms were consistently being ejected at an odd angle, which made the machine jam and caused severe damage to the inner workings. Upon notification, the factory inspected the units and discovered the problem was a bent shaft, which was duly replaced. A quality control station was set up temporarily to replace any bent shafts that were found on the production line. Several weeks passed and once again, complaints came pouring in from the field; the units were again ejecting the forms incorrectly and creating malfunctions. Again, the problem was bent shafts. Where were they coming from? It turned out that a young man, who was hired to sweep up and generally clean the area behind the assembly line, came upon a bin which was serving as a repository for the bad shafts. He recognized them as being like the ones being installed down the line, so he picked them up, took them back down the line and put them on the shelf with new parts! Proper training and communication could have prevented this.

We spend 30 to 35 percent of our time doing things over again. IBM did a study in their own company and in August of 1990 stated they were spending 30 percent of their time doing things over. Let's examine another giant of the '60's, Xerox. David Kearns and David Nadler, in their book, *Prophets in the Dark: How Xerox Reinvented Itself and Beat Back the Japanese* (Harper Business, 1992), reported that in October, 1982, the company dropped a bomb to begin the quality process. Kearns says, "Probably the most dramatic piece of information we divulged was our conviction that the lack of quality at Xerox was costing the company a whopping $1.4 billion a year. That number got everyone's attention in a hurry."

We talk about the national debt as being a tragedy; but the real tragedy in America is that even in some of our best companies, 30 to 35 percent of our time is spent

doing it over!

This is a terrible loss of time, talent and treasure. Nobody likes to do things over. Do you know the expression, "The hurrier I go, the behinder I get"? Doing things over uses time that could be spent more productively; and pushing employees to do their usual work *and* do things over, causes them to try to work faster, with, perhaps, even *more* errors. Quality is taking pains to do it right the first time. If we totally eliminated having to do things over, think of the additional products we could make in the 30 to 35 percent more time we'd have. The increased inventory would add to the bottom line with no expenditure for more people or equipment.

Thirty to thirty-five percent means *one-third* of our time is spent doing things over. If you looked at this in your personal life, it would be like losing eight hours a day. Or, suppose someone took one-third of your salary and threw it in the trash? This is after taxes, by the way. Is that okay with you?

Many years ago a Xerox advertising campaign boasted, "If our copier breaks, we'll have it fixed within four hours." But the Japanese were quietly building copiers that didn't break so often.

Some people say, "We just buy Japanese cars because they're cheaper." If you think they're cheaper, you haven't priced a 300ZX lately. They are not necessarily cheaper, but they're perceived to be better. We buy them because we want cars to run dependably. In other words, we want quality. Ford and Chrysler, and lately General Motors in its Saturn Division, are finally beginning to get this message; but the automobile industry is not the only one fighting for survival today.

QUALITY IS FREE (It Isn't; it's Profitable)

"Quality is not only right, it's free. And it's not only free, but it's the most profitable product we have." So said Harold Geneen of I.T.T., and *Quality is Free* (McGraw-Hill, 1979) was the title of Philip B. Crosby's book, one of the first to define quality as "conformance to requirements." In an interview by Paul Burnham Finney in a recent issue of *Management Digest*, Crosby said, "Back in 1961 when I was at Martin (Martin-Marietta Corp.), I came up with the concept of zero defects... A few years later I went over to ITT and became the first vice-president of quality ever appointed in a corporation. ...Harold Geneen, the man who ran the show, was the first to understand zero defects... The grand old men of business ridiculed it. They thought it was naive. God had proclaimed that statistically it was impossible to achieve zero defects.

"...It's not just finding the disease and curtailing it, but never getting the disease at all. ... If an organization doesn't do what it says it will do, it's going to die. ... When Japanese had low wages and products at low prices, American companies were spending 25 percent of their revenue to do things over. That's in manufacturing. In the service industries, they spend 40 percent.... At one time, for every one defect in Japanese cars, there were 15 in American cars. ... Everybody leaped on quality circles as a motivational tool. They thought that quality was, at heart, a worker problem. Instead it's a problem of policy. Educating an entire company to do things right. ...we focused on the four absolutes: conformance to requirements, prevention, zero defects and the price of nonconformance.... You really have to change your company so it runs on the basis of integrity."

In one respect the skeptics were right about zero defects. If products are machined or worked on in any way, getting all of them to be perfectly alike is virtually impossible. But a very slight tolerance from perfection will not have a significant effect on the end result. Therefore, zero defects came to mean that a product was within a certain tolerance of the ideal, say 0.01 percent off. Americans had no problem conforming to that standard when it was implemented in many factories around the country. And, as long as the tolerance was met, they congratulated themselves on having "zero defects."

However, when the Japanese workers were given the same standards, differences began to show up. The Japanese didn't aim to be within the tolerance level; they aimed for the ideal. When both Ford and Mazda were producing identical parts, it was discovered that more of the Mazda parts were close to the ideal parameters than Ford's. Not enough to make a difference, you say? After all, they met the tolerance requirements, you say? But, minuscule deviations have a way of piling up. If every part in a particular component of an automobile is at the outside edge of its tolerance, that component's chances of not performing properly escalate. More of these components were performing poorly or breaking down, and the work

had to be done over.

The cost of improving quality is always less than the cost of doing things over. There are direct costs of doing things wrong, such as honoring service warranties on faulty products, the training of field service personnel, even possible lawsuits resulting from product failures. In addition, there are less obvious costs, such as lost time, slow payments because customers are dissatisfied, extra material to make the repairs, extra paper work by office staff, engineering expenses to redesign a product, to say nothing of loss of future business because most dissatisfied customers—who may never tell you why!—will refuse to buy from you again.

Clearly, we must tell our staff, employees, all workers, in fact, what their function is; be certain they know, not allow them to guess at it. Most importantly, we must tell our people—from the senior officers to the newest trainee—exactly who their personal customers are inside the organization, the recipients of their job effort, no matter what its nature. Then we can look for reduced errors, increased profits, satisfied customers and pride in our organization. Then and only then will we have true quality, the ultimate profit.

Unless we do this, the scenario, familiar to all Americans who watched the loss of revenue because of offshore product superiority, can and will repeat itself. The service industry will be the next to be overtaken by foreign ownership and management and we must act now to turn the tide.

In *American Business: a Two Minute Warning*, by C. Jackson Grayson, Jr. and Carla O'Dell, (The Free Press, 1988) the authors—after many years of experience gauging productivity in American business—warn us that: "(1) U.S. competitiveness has seriously eroded, (2) the international competitive challenges are far stronger than most people yet realize, (3) the U.S. response to date is inadequate to meet the challenges, and (4) not only *can* the

United States lose its world economic leadership, but at the moment it *is* losing."

What this means to the country as a whole—besides losing its 100-year position as number one in the world—is that there will be less and less money, even with higher taxes, to solve our education, health, crime and other problems; and, for individuals, that their standard of living will continue to shrink. Real weekly earnings are already lower than they were in 1962. Using the value of 1986 dollars, in 1973 a thirty-year-old American male earned over $25,000 per year; today it's only $18,000, and continues to decline.

A hundred years ago, when England was the dominant economic force in the world, articles and books warned them that they were losing competitiveness and productivity, but no one listened. Soon the United States replaced England in that role. Today, we stand at the same crossroads. There are no more time outs; will we listen and heed the warning?

INTERVIEW with L.A. LABEL

Jim Valestrino, president of L.A. Label, inherited his business. It was a family-held corporation and grew from five employees to over 60; but he describes the way it was run during the '50's and '60's as a fast and furious operation with not much thought about reruns or wasted material and effort. When he took over from his father, he ran it that way too for awhile but was dissatisfied. He wasn't happy going to work every morning and he sensed that the employees weren't happy either. But how to change things?

"About six or seven years ago," Jim says, "I realized that the employees were caring and wanted to do a good job and build a quality product; but because of our economy and our culture, direction was missing, and it was up to me to provide

*direction. I wanted the company to expand, but I also wanted
a better company environment.*

*"We were increasing sales, but not profits. We were also
losing 20 percent of our old customers, because growing
competition—both at home and abroad—started to penetrate
our industry. We knew we were losing money through doing
a lot of things over, but, since we didn't measure anything, we
had no real idea of the extent of the loss.*

*"In addition, we had a serious tardy and absentee problem
and some substance abuse among employees. And we had
turnover of at least 25 percent a year. We had company
benefits, like medical and profit sharing, but no rewards or
incentives for doing a quality job or coming up with good
suggestions. In fact, morale in the company was poor. The
employees were afraid to speak out and the managers were
afraid of any change from the way they had always done
things.*

*"I tried to improve the system, but the problem when you
make a change from one style of management to another is
that doing it yourself is difficult. People don't always believe
in your motives. I recognized the need to have an outside
service come in and start the ball rolling. I hired Quality
Concepts, because it was obvious our change was about
quality: quality of product and quality of operations. We had
to make the employees understand what we were trying to do
and then have independent evaluations, so they wouldn't be
afraid of repercussions.*

*"I also realized it had to be on-going. You don't change
things overnight. That's one of the basic tenets of Quality
Concepts. The other two are to hold in-house workshops
dealing with our issues, and that those had to involve everyone in the company. When the managers sit down with them
and listen to the same message, the employees can see that
the company is really serious about the process. "*

Jim had learned that the old management style bred lack
of trust. Employees were worked long hours and pushed to do
even more. Management didn't share the vision of the
company for the future; the old style was to tell employees

nothing. They were afraid some of them might start their own, similar, business and become unwanted competition. "But you can't live in fear of what people may do while you're helping them improve.

"Too many managers still feel that quality is something you have a right to expect from the guy on the floor, the people making the label; but it's not. It begins and ends with management. Every manager at L.A. Label had to be brought into the philosophy of what I wanted to do. It wasn't easy. It took about a year to get managers over their fear, because people are reluctant to change. Change creates doubt and insecurity. They had to learn that change can be a good thing and that it fosters growth, not loss."

Jim says, "We perform annual management surveys and annual employee surveys. The managers review one another and the employees review management. Because they're confidential, people can be honest in reporting and this information shows what's been accomplished and where there are areas for improvement.

"This process has led to many changes in the way we produce our labels. For one thing, we now keep track of rejects and categorize them. If a job was done incorrectly, we take great pains to research why it happened, and instead of blaming anyone, we have a mini-workshop to teach how to do it right.

"We have weekly management meetings and good ideas come out of them. We have no quality control or inspection crew; no one is hanging around surreptitiously trying to detect screw-ups. We spend our time looking for opportunities to improve rather than looking for mistakes. We found that people started taking pride in their work and did a better job. They made suggestions and it had a snowball effect.

"One of the most important changes we made was to institute what we call Ready Meetings. When we have a complicated job, we call in everyone involved and may spend up to two hours ironing out all the details in advance. We learned that it's a lot less expensive and more productive to spend that time up front, rather than letting a day-and-a-half *job escalate to three days or more because you had to rerun it due to errors.*

"Our biggest focus is on developing and utilizing ideas from all employees. We now get them involved and develop creativity which leads to new ideas and new products. Best of all, out of this has come an unbelievable amount of support for our customers. We've had people in the shipping department help customers in ways we never thought of. One maintenance man was repairing a fence and saw a customer loading his car and he went over and helped. Before our Quality Concepts workshops, he'd never have done that. Some customers have gone out of their way to tell us they like our value-added focus.

"More than that, it's created an environment where people actually like to come to work. Absenteeism has dropped dramatically. There is virtually no turnover. We changed the way we hire employees. We used to look for people who had experience and could run a certain machine; now we look for people with creativity, a willingness to learn and a team spirit."

Jim has been able to add a 401K plan for his employees; but he's done more than add benefits and instill a quality perspective in his employees. He continually finds ways to help them in their private lives as well. For example, he foots the bill for activities during non-working hours at his plant, activities such as CPR training, emergency fire procedures by the local fire department, and earthquake safety techniques. He even hires teachers for employees who are lacking in language skills. Birthdays, weddings, new babies and personal accomplishments are recognized, creating a family of employees who work together and support one another and the organization.

Jim Valestrino is a very tough competitor who makes quality pay off!

Quality is knowing you're the best in your field, yet feeling the need to improve.

Robert D. Sherer

6

WHAT IS "IT"?

Success is a journey, not a destination.
Ben Sweetland

I am not saying that all American workers are incapable of doing quality work. There are plenty who have never made a serious mistake in their lives. I've been married for 35 years to a person like that. Sometimes she tells me she can't understand how I can make a living talking about this. She says, "Why wouldn't people just naturally do things right the first time? Wouldn't it be simpler?" And I say, "Yes, but not everybody is like you." So if you're perfect already, like my wife, this may be hard for you to understand, but bear with me.

If part of the definition of quality is communicating to understand the requirements of the job and doing it right the first time to the customer's satisfaction, then our next concern must be, "What is 'it'?"

There are bumper stickers that say, "Accountants Do It by the Book" or even, "Bikers Do It in the Dirt." The joke comes in the cleverness (or lack of same) in matching the occupation to whatever you think "it" is. But in business, if you don't know what "it" is, your chances of doing it right the first time are two: slim and none.

Accuracy, then momentum, is the path that leads to higher quality and profits. Unfortunately, too many people, when faced with a task, choose momentum first, instead of accuracy. Accuracy is achieved by studying, analyzing and deciding what exactly has to be done. Only then have you defined the big "it."

What does quality mean to you? Maybe you know it when you see it. Maybe it's a product built to last, a product that works like it's supposed to. It's a job well done. It's correct and on time. It gives you a feeling of satisfaction and integrity.

One of our oldest adages is, "If you build a better mousetrap, the world will beat a path to your door." Yet, when American businesses first realized that products made in other countries were better, cheaper and would usually be delivered on time, they tried many ways, other than building a better product, to try to recapture the market. They tried cutting salaries of their workers, asked unions for concessions, in hopes of keeping down costs; they exhorted the schools to do a better job of education; they cried that Congress must reduce the federal deficit; they even suggested a cabinet-level Department of Business and Technology. You'd think they had no idea that doing it right the first time was the missing ingredient.

In fact, thanks to the Japanese, the Deming Prize, the Malcolm Baldrige Award, and others, the world is moving so rapidly in this direction, that people are beginning to expect, not just quality, but a value that exceeds their expectations. Price is still a consideration, but they also want on-time delivery and exceptional service and reliability.

THE MULTI-BILLION-DOLLAR DEVICE

It's been said that there are three kinds of people in the world:

- People who make things happen.
- People who watch things happen.
- People who wonder what happened.

Sometimes I think we need to add another: People who don't know that anything happened!

We've tended to become a nation of people who watch things happen, but don't want to get involved. If someone in our company has a problem, do we go over and help, or do we watch it happen and move away so it won't tarnish us?

Not getting involved can lead to disaster. The destruction of the Challenger space shuttle and loss of the crew a few years ago need never have happened. The engineers said that the O-rings couldn't work properly at temperatures of 39 degrees or less. But nobody listened. The Hubbell telescope, which had a serious flaw, was built by two different companies *who didn't talk to each other*. So we spent billions of dollars for something that wasn't right and then another billion or so to fix it.

Who are the people who make things happen? Management? Yes. Employees? Yes. *Everybody* makes things happen in a high performance company. If management means responsibility, then everyone is a manager, because every worker is responsible for something.

Inside your head is a multi-billion dollar device. We call it a brain. It's more powerful than any computer. As a matter of fact, we don't even know how powerful this thing is. We haven't been able to make an instrument to measure the ultimate capability of the human mind. The good news is that everybody comes equipped with one! What's the bad news? Right. Some can't find the "on" switch.

How much of this device do we use? Scientists think we probably use only 10 percent of it. Albert Einstein once said that he didn't use more than 10 percent of his mind, so think how much less the rest of us are using. On her popular television show, Roseanne, when informed by her friend Crystal that "we only use 2 percent of our brains," responded, "That much, huh?"

Whether you're the lowliest man on the corporate totem pole or the chairman of the board, you make decisions every day that affect your job and your life with your own Multi-Billion Dollar Device. Nobody does it for you.

Some time after World War II, along with losing the work ethic, many Americans began to externalize. They blamed everyone else for whatever happened to them. This was exacerbated by the proliferation of psychiatrists, psychologists and therapists who eschewed guilt and looked for causes of your anti-social behavior in your past experiences. It was no longer your fault. It was your mother's fault, or your teacher's, or the moon or the government. (But at least we can't blame the Soviet Union anymore.) So we stopped taking responsibility and didn't bother to find the switch to turn on our billion-dollar device.

SETTING GOALS

How can we use the billion-dollar device? By setting goals. There's a saying, "If you don't know where you're going, any road will get you there." However, I've updated this to: "If you don't know where you're going, you might as well pull off, 'cause you're not going anywhere." Sometimes we know what our goals are and work toward them. At other times we don't consciously think about them; but what we do—or fail to do—shows the world clearly where we're headed. You need to ask yourself if that's where you really want to go.

Thoreau said, "The mass of men lead lives of quiet desperation." I've often thought that what most of them actually do is "ad lib" their way through life. Thomas La Mance has said, "Life is what happens to us while we are making other plans." Many people don't plan their future; it just happens to them. Many make no plans at all. They have only the vaguest notion of what their future should be like and how to get there.

What are some of your goals in life? What do you want? Education, marriage, children, to buy a house, win the lottery, retire? The bottom line is: you can't do any of these things without money, and that means you have to earn, steal or inherit money. Fortunately, most of us get to earn it. When we first start out in the work force, sometimes it never occurs to us that we're going to be doing this for a long, long time, perhaps for the rest of our lives. Therefore, you'd better find and turn on the switch to your billion-dollar device early.

Quality of life only occurs if you keep putting information into your billion-dollar device. There's a computer saying, Garbage In, Garbage Out. If you put garbage into your billion-dollar device, garbage is what's going to come out. What are *you* putting in your computer brain? Some people use the time while driving in their cars to listen to loud rock music. Others tune in all-news stations so they know what's going on in the world. Still others listen to books on tape, or turn off the noise entirely just to think about their current work and their future.

It's been said that your best thinking is done by your subconscious mind, and it can work while you're asleep. If you're wrestling with a problem and sleep on it, your subconscious will sift through all the data you stored there during your waking hours and may come up with a solution for you. But it only happens if there's something in there to work on, if you put in some worthwhile data to begin with. What you put into your multi-billion dollar device is what you're really about.

How do you get to the goals you aspire to? Write them down. There are no wrong answers, but the best ones come out the end of your finger. But be sure you spend some time actively thinking—turning on your billion-dollar device—to figure out ways you can make those dreams come true.

A story is told about two men talking about their future, and one said to the other, "I'm going to go to college and get a degree; then I can get a job in the field I'm interested in."

The other said, "That's okay for you. But I'm older. Four years from now I'll be 30. I don't want to spend the time."

His friend replied, "But four years from now you're going to be 30 anyway. If you go to college, you'll be 30 and have a degree too."

Turning on your brain/computer is a little like being in a car driving down the highway of life, and you need to have your headlights turned on. That's why you must write down your goals and look at them. Are they realistic? What steps do you have to take to reach your goals? Don't rely on luck to make them happen. There's a saying, "The harder I work, the luckier I get." Yes, opportunity knocks once in a while, but you won't recognize it if you don't have your lights turned on, if you're not at the proper door, if you haven't prepared yourself to recognize the opportunity when it presents itself.

There are people on the highway of life who have *no* lights turned on. They want *you* to fail because they aren't going anywhere themselves and you make them look bad. They have no goals and they'll keep you from getting to *your* goals if they can. You have a birthright to feel good about yourself and they try to spoil it. They interfere with your work, waste your time, or suggest you go drinking together, or offer you drugs. If your own lights are turned on, you'll recognize these people for what they are: O.B.T.'s, On-Board Terrorists. Sadly, many companies have them, and it's up to you to recognize them and not let them terrorize *you*.

On a work day, you're going to spend more of your waking hours at your job than you will with your family at home. Doesn't it make sense to make those the best you can? If you take responsibility for what you do and how you do it, you'll not only increase the likelihood of earning more money and reaching your goals, but you'll be happier along the way. Life is short and we need to enjoy it, not just at home after work, but all day long.

When we practice quality in our jobs, we protect them. If we do things wrong and have to do them over, it only comes back to hit us in the wallet. Whose money was lost? Ours. It's next year's raise, the new car, the vacation with the kids. It's the company's new health insurance program. It's our pension for retirement. If it costs money to do things over again, there will be less for bonuses and for expansion. The company may even disintegrate and the jobs will disappear.

INTERVIEW with WINTER FINANCIAL GROUP

Not all quality problems involve tangible products, manufactured blivets. Even a service company can experience the loss that occurs when employees must do-it-over-again. Such a company was Winter Financial Group, a financial planning company with both individual and corporate clients.

As Larry Winter, president, said in a recent interview, "We were definitely doing things over and I don't know if we even realized that was a quality issue. We weren't managing the business properly; we were just doing things by trial and error. When Quality Concepts came in, they started talking about setting goals. This caught my attention because I had heard a talk about setting 101 lifetime goals.

"This sounds almost impossible, but it isn't. Many motivational speakers will tell you to set ten goals, say millionaire, guru of this or president of that. Those are goals you may accomplish, but it can be discouraging because there's no way you can accomplish them in less than five or ten years, or even more! But if you're going to write down 101 lifetime goals, some will be short-term—that you might reach next week or next month—and they should be not only career, but financial, spiritual, physical, mental, family-centered and so on.

"Writing down these goals is important, but it's also exciting; and Bob Sherer reminded us to look at the list of goals at least once a week, to update it monthly and to check off the items that you accomplish. I probably have 250 goals written down and when I get up in the morning I can look at my goal chart and know what I'm going to work on that day. Little things can give you big rewards."

Larry says he hired Quality Concepts to provide guidance in his goal for quality service and he thinks employees "will listen more to a person who is an expert in quality, for instance, versus someone who may be their manager but who is an expert only at selling investments."

Once a quarter Larry reviews all staff members. He talks with them and learns what they've done in the last quarter in the areas of quality of their work, education, attitude, time management and trying to find better ways to do things. They get bonuses based on their performance in these areas. "When we first started the process," Winter says, "there was a little bit of fear that there was going to be change. Some people are almost terrified of change. But Quality Concepts programs are very reassuring and non-threatening and they learn that improving quality is definitely a benefit to them in the long run."

Winter Financial Group doesn't have a suggestion box system, but one of the unanticipated benefits of the quality process is that employees now feel free to bring up suggestions and concerns at the weekly Monday morning meetings. Rather than a waste of time, the meetings are short and focused on what needs to be done. Even if the managers don't attend the meetings—and often they can't because of client appointments—the employees discuss which goals should be met that week and how they'll meet them.

"Recently, we've been holding some lunches with clients where we ask them why they do business with us, and the number one reason is trust. I feel that we've earned that trust as a result of what we've learned about setting lifetime goals and striving for quality."

ALONE IN THE DARK

Henry Ford had a lot to do with the American manufacturing revolution when he was building the first Ford automobiles. Before then, only the wealthiest people had cars because they were expensive. We were a nation of craftspeople, and automobiles were made by hand, one at a time. But Henry Ford invented the assembly line, which dramatically cut the cost of producing cars. Instead of one person making the entire car, each person did just one small thing. Like stick a bolt in a hole. If a hole came by on the assembly line, you stuck a bolt in it. No hole, no bolt. That's it; don't think. Turn off your craftsmanship lights.

That was a revolutionary idea, because people who previously lived on farms had done everything for themselves. They built their own houses and barns, grew their food, made their own clothes. It was gratifying to know that ordinary people could now afford cars, but we traded something for that. We developed a lot of people who didn't think anymore, people who watched things happen, who turned off their lights.

In some companies—not just automobile companies, but all kinds of manufacturing operations—workers sometimes did more than just stick bolts in holes and watch things happen. It took five or ten minutes to train new employees to do that and about the same amount of time for them to become bored stupid. Because the job was boring, their minds sometimes went to sleep; and being human, they occasionally made mistakes. When a mistake was found, and someone came to the line to find out who was to blame, Jenny, who put bolts in fender holes, blamed Joe, next to her who gave her the fender, or Moe, who tightened the bolt. That didn't make Joe or Moe happy and one day Moe drew a chalk line on the floor and said to Jenny, "Don't step over this line."

Then Joe said, "Oh yeah, well I'm going to build a wall between us, so you can't even look at me!" And pretty soon, no one spoke to anyone else. There was no team at work to build the cars, just individuals who didn't care what happened down the line; it wasn't their responsibility. We all know the story of the man seated in the restaurant, who flags down a passing waiter and asks him what time it is. The waiter replies, "This isn't my table." That's funny, but what isn't funny is the proliferation of people who take that attitude. In his book, *It's Not My Department* (W. Morrow, 1990), Peter Glen gives dozens of examples of this kind of behavior that alienates customers, drives costs up, and ultimately can close down a business forever. And not just a service-oriented business. Any business will go under if the workers don't work together.

The Japanese have taught us, with their quality circles and *kaizen*, that teamwork is one key to success. Groups of workers come up with better ideas, because there are more minds at work on a problem. The old fashioned production line has become obsolete. We need to teach workers to do several related tasks, not one narrow job. This cross-trained team concept is already working in many U.S. companies, such as Xerox, Rohm & Haas, and Tektronix, Inc.

Writing in the *Christian Science Monitor* about the new work systems at LTV Steel, Laurent Belsie said, "Instead of a thick labor contract that spells out rules, union and management have negotiated a 25-page document that defines goals. Worker-manager teams resolve disputes and set performance criteria. Worker teams interview and select the company's new hires and figure out how to schedule themselves. Instead of hundreds of job classifications, the new unit has only four." Technicians there report that they are no longer bored by what they do, because every day is different and they're always learning something new.

MEASUREMENT (Scoreboarding)

The managers who build quality teams in their companies must set the right example. Most quality problems are *not* the result of errors by production employees; a significant percentage are the result of errors by management, such as poor decisions or failure to ensure that various departments work together harmoniously. Low employee morale can lead to poor results, and it is managers who are responsible for the morale of employees. Give them training, the proper tools, an explanation of the requirements, and a team spirit and, in time, higher quality productivity and profits will be the result.

One of the best tools for instituting quality programs in business is the survey. When surveys of employees and managers are compared, problems that hinder quality production often show up. Peter Drucker says, "What gets measured, gets done." You can't fix a problem if you don't know what it is. Even the dumpster emptying schedule will tell you a lot about what's going on in your company.

The sample survey on page 72 is a good start toward finding out. The first measurement is how many employees will respond. Obviously if you send out 100 employee surveys and get none back, it might offer a clue about trust and fear. Or everyone's so happy they didn't want to tell you.

An article in *Business Week* pointed out that "quality exists between the customer's ears." Management consultant Ann Coplin, expanding on this idea, says, "As part of our efforts to insure customer satisfaction, we must first determine customers' needs (both stated and unstated) and then establish measurements that will enable us to accurately determine how well we are fulfilling those needs...

"Many of the measurements used today are meaningless. We often see measures that were created a long time ago to serve someone else's need. They don't reflect the customer's view-point...

"Begin by developing a corporate mission statement and sharing it with all your people... Solicit feedback from prime customers through surveys, questionnaires, toll-free phone lines and in-person interviews... Audit internal suppliers as well... Schedule meetings to review measurement results... If you are communicating results with written reports, keep them simple and informative and share them with everybody....remember, you are measuring for improvement, not for show and tell."

We recommend that departments set up scoreboards to communicate how they're doing. These are very effective mea-surement tools and the company leaders can readily see what's happening in those departments ("management by walking around"). Some people get very creative with their scoreboards. During a tour of U.S.A.A. Insurance in San Antonio, Texas, I saw

INTERNAL CUSTOMER SATISFACTION SURVEY

BELOW MY EXPECTATIONS		MEETS MY EXPECTATIONS			EXCEEDS MY EXPECTATIONS	
1	2	3	4	5	6	7

USING THE ABOVE SCALE, PLEASE CIRCLE ONE NUMBER INDICATING HOW YOU RATE THE FOLLOWING: COMMENTS ARE ENCOURAGED. HOW CAN IT BE IMPROVED? PLEASE BE AS SPECIFIC AS POSSIBLE.

YOUR RATING

1. How is the company doing at "Doing it Right the First Time?"   1 2 3 4 5 6 7

2. How open are the lines of communication within the company?   1 2 3 4 5 6 7

3. How is the quality of communication between you and your manager?   1 2 3 4 5 6 7

4. How would you rate the trust and respect you get from your manager?   1 2 3 4 5 6 7

5. How well does your manager communicate goals and objectives?   1 2 3 4 5 6 7

6. How would you rate the training you receive?   1 2 3 4 5 6 7

7. How would you rate the recognition you receive?   1 2 3 4 5 6 7

8. How do you feel about your physical work space?   1 2 3 4 5 6 7

9. How do you feel about the teamwork in your department?   1 2 3 4 5 6 7

10. How do you feel about your employee benefit and incentive programs?   1 2 3 4 5 6 7

11. How would you rate the compensation you receive for the work you do?   1 2 3 4 5 6 7

12. How would you rate your opportunity for career advancement in your company?   1 2 3 4 5 6 7

(CONTINUED ON NEXT PAGE)

13. How do you rate the pride and accomplishment you feel from your work?   1 2 3 4 5 6 7

_____

14. How would you rate your overall satisfaction as an employee of your company?   1 2 3 4 5 6 7

_____

15. What do you need in order to do a better job for your internal and external customers?

*comments:*_____

_____

_____

16. What's needed in order for the company to become a better place to work?

*comments:*_____

_____

_____

17. Other comments - good or bad - are welcome!

*comments:*_____

_____

_____

_____

_____

_____

Thanks for your valued feedback!
QUALITY CONCEPTS

boards that were kept up by employees, including the dates for quality team meetings, that almost shouted out how they were performing. You think employees aren't capable of keeping score? They know the stats on their favorite teams and players, don't they?

ETHICS

The "It" of quality is also ethics. Only our personal ethical standards separate us from the criminal behind bars. Before you dismiss this section because you already behave in an ethical manner, think about one business tool that Henry Ford never had to worry about: the computer. Examine your computer practices, and those of your contemporaries. Consider some serious problems that have arisen lately due to computer technology.

Newspapers reported not long ago that a graduate student at Cornell University introduced a program into a gigantic computer network, causing 6,000 computers—used by government agencies and universities—to lose incredible amounts of stored memory, and therefore millions of dollars in time and wages. In 1992, millions of personal computer users were forced to protect themselves from a virus called Michaelangelo that could wipe out all their data. The Software Publishers Association recently found over 500 copies of software programs that had been obtained illegally.

Why do people, who wouldn't dream of pilfering something from the local five-and-dime, steal (by copying) a $300 software program? As computers and their users multiply, these and similar questions arise daily, perhaps because such "stealing" is unique in that the original remains with its owner. The same is true of reproducing, via copy machines found on any street in America, someone else's written words. Ethically, these practices are just as wrong as a child taking a toy without paying for it. Not everyone makes his living producing a blivet; some write software programs and some write books, articles and music. The only way they can keep making their mortgage payments is when they're paid for their work; to use it without permission is theft. Unfortunately, advances in technology have made it easy for some people to trample on the rights of others, whether it's their work or their privacy.

"In 1986, Digital Equipment Company conducted a study on the possible effects of semiconductor assembly on pregnant women. When the study revealed that this work could increase the possibility of miscarriage, DEC published the results and encouraged..." (not forced) "...women to transfer to lower-risk positions - *at their current pay* (italics added)." This respect for employees is just one of the reasons DEC has been recognized as a good place to work.

More and more corporate officers are beginning to realize that not everyone comes to work with a desire to do the right thing for its own sake. Although it's reported that Harvard and many other schools are now teaching the subject, too many college graduates never took a course in integrity or ethical business practices. Cheating scandals have rocked some of our best universities. A report compiled by the California-based Josephson Institute of Ethics and reported in the March, 1996, issue of *Readers Digest*, found that as many as 75 percent of high school students admit to cheating; for college students, 50 percent is common. *U.S. News and World Report* asked young adults if there were some circumstances that justified stealing from an employer. Thirty-four percent said yes.

It therefore behooves management to see that integrity and ethics are part of the rules and regulations of their work place; that management and employees are expected to behave ethically at all times. From a purely practical standpoint, it's a necessity; because employees who believe they've been unfairly treated quit their jobs, or, even worse, may sabotage their employers with shoddy work, disruptive customer attitudes or unethical practices of their own. Severely disgruntled employees, as you've heard on the evening news, have been known to return to the workplace with automatic weapons and shoot everyone in sight.

For years the business dinner, three-martini lunch and power breakfast, all on someone else's expense account, have been taken for granted; but lately some companies are questioning the ethics of letting suppliers provide perks that may lead to cries of influence buying or discrimination from competitors. Some companies have forbidden purchasing agents to accept even the smallest of gratuities lest they be construed as bribes.

A company that is serious about maintaining an ethical image must not only see that its highest officers know what the policy is and adhere to it; but they must be sure every employee in the company follows it as well. It needs to be written in the company manual, and mentioned during preliminary interviews with new recruits, as well as performance evaluations. To reinforce the policy, managers may give praise, raises or bonuses, and publish the names of exemplary individuals in their newsletters or on bulletin boards.

The list of socially responsible companies—companies which practice product quality, environmental responsibility, participatory management, equal opportunity employment and work-place safety, while avoiding connections with alcohol, tobacco, nuclear power, gambling and weapons manufacturing—is growing and more investors are moving their money into those stocks. There now exist a dozen stock mutual funds that invest only in such companies. In fact, as reported in *Money Magazine*, such funds, far from penalizing their investors, do better than others.

For example, while the Dow Jones Industrial Average plunged 24 percent during its one-day slide on Black Monday in October, 1987, Pax, Calvert and New Alternatives—all socially responsible funds—dropped an average of only 8 percent. By the end of the year they had posted gains, not losses. For the five years ending December 1990, four out of five of the ethical mutual funds in business since 1986 posted gains four to 13 percentage points higher than that of other funds. Lipper Analytical Services rated Working Assets Balanced Fund as the number one performer in the three months ending October 31, 1992.

Ethics in business is necessary for survival, because customers who think they've been cheated soon find other sources of supply. Not to mention that such activities can create lawsuits, penalties and a soiled company reputation.

For 35 years, Robert W. Dingman has been at the top of his field, executive recruiting. Bob's successful career is ethics centered. Building a high-performing business, acting as board member and leader of academic and business institutions and volunteering his time and talent to a hospice are evidence of Bob's ethical nature and service to people.

The Robert W. Dingman Company of Westlake Village, CA, publishes a newsletter, "Reflections from the Lamp." In a recent issue, Bob spoke to the question of ethics:

> *"Ethics is a term that can mean 'how the race is run,' and it is a subject of concern to me, both in general and as it applies to my profession. The evidence is overwhelming that not everyone is equally concerned. Honda had a dozen of its American executives imprisoned for running a bribery and kickback scheme. The judge commented, 'Everyone has their eyes on money instead of a very simple and basic understanding of what is right and what is wrong.' What could serve as a clearer definition of 'having no ethical standards'?"*

The Japanese may not be more ethical than we are, but they are certainly less adversarial. Just as they use teams and consensus to solve working problems, they are far less litigious. They prefer to handle conflicts by compromise based on trust and common fate. Grayson and O'Dell, in *American Business: A Two Minute Warning*, point out that one study showed that, out of over 2500 taxicab accidents in Tokyo, only two lawsuits were filed, and barely 2 percent of divorces end up in court. Japan has fewer than 80,000 lawyers and other legal personnel; the U.S. has about 700,000, two-thirds of all the lawyers in the world. And our law schools are choked with future lawyers.

One of the reasons many people give for the low ethical standards of our politicians is that most of them are attorneys. Comic Jay Leno gets wild applause when he likens them to Saddam Hussein or to sharks, because the public has a justifiably low image of lawyers. So it came as a pleasant surprise to read a recent article in *Time* Magazine by Emily Mitchell that Michael Josephson, a former law professor at Loyola Marymount University in Los Angeles, who began teaching ethics in 1976, is now getting increasing numbers of calls to teach ethics classes to hundreds of companies and organizations, one of which is the New York State Bar Association.

In 1990, California voters passed an ethics reform bill which makes attendance at such courses mandatory for all legislators and their staffs, and Josephson is "optimistic that every leading business ... organization will have an ethics-education program. 'Without it,' he warns,' they are going to get chewed up from inside and outside.' In fact, the ethics movement will be to the '90's what the consumer movement was to the '60's."

Virtue may be its own reward, but ethical conduct is quality business practice and brings its rewards to the bottom line.

Challenge: What can you do to provide goals, measurement and ethics in your organization?

_____

_____

_____

_____

_____

_____

_____

7

DECISIONS

*Developing character and vision is the way
leaders invent themselves.*

Warren Bennis

J unk is a four-letter word. We can't say it too often: quality
begins with honesty, integrity and operating in an ethical
manner. More and more, as we travel the road of leadership
and organizational development, we learn that junk bonds, flim-
flam operations, and taking advantage of others—be it customers
or employees—not only doesn't pay off, but in fact destroys
companies, careers and the moral fiber of America. It's time we
changed the way we make decisions and do business.

INTERVIEW with TRIWEST INSURANCE

*"Two and a half years ago," states Paul Bronow, president
of Triwest Insurance, a multiple-line insurance agency located
in Sherman Oaks, California, "we were considerably different
from who and what we are today. Triwest was a composite
of two agencies doing business in a cluster arrangement. We
were two small family-oriented businesses with different
purposes and different cultures. Today, we are one agency
with a considerably different culture and new responsibilities.
My purpose, two and a half years ago, was to live a comfortable life and manage the agency to a profitable bottom line.
I now understand that my responsibility is to empower my
employees for success."*

*Paul's focus with his company of only thirty employees
was as a salesman first; he admits he had a rather cavalier*

attitude toward his responsibilities as the president of the firm. His purpose was to increase sales, provide a professional service for his clients, and to create a profit. The overnight increase in the size of the business, by virtue of the consolidation of the two cluster agencies, forced him to take a new, hard look at the structure, the processes and the responsibilities for the management of the agency. In addition to those issues, the insurance industry was changing and competition was increasing. Paul knew productivity had to improve, "doing things over" had to be reduced; but he recognized he didn't have the tools to institute these changes himself. He recognized that the advantages of outside help would not only be the most effective use of his time, but would also shortcut the process.

"What intrigued me about Quality Concepts," states Mr. Bronow, "was the humanistic approach—that it's more than just charts and measurement—it's actually a cultural issue and Quality Concepts recognized that concept."

Paul says, "I had a management team of individuals who were technically competent but didn't have specific training in management, leadership and communication, what Bob Sherer calls the people side of quality. They were a group of strong-willed individuals, all of whom had an intention to get a job done."

Thanks to leadership training workshops, a year later the trust, communication and focus of the leader team had been strengthened, resulting in a cohesive group working together with a clear direction and purpose.

Paul had used employee surveys, which he says became a "reality check" for him. He said "I always thought I was a great communicator but, through the surveys, I learned that I lacked certain communication skills." To help remedy this situation, the agency created an agency newsletter that provides information to employees about all aspects of the business. Recent newsletter issues acknowledged employees who had provided especially good service for clients or other departments.

Triwest also has regular employee evaluations, providing all employees with a review of their personal progress. The agency provides incentives and bonuses, and has created a career development program where they promote and hire from within. They have also established salary grids, thereby creating a higher level of satisfaction and a sense of fairness. Triwest is becoming known as a good place to work.

"When we started our suggestion box," states Paul, "we were getting self-serving recommendations. But, now, thanks to the Quality Concepts programs and improved communication, employees are better focused. As a result, we now receive suggestions that are meaningful recommendations for the improvement of quality and efficiency of the entire agency." The success of this effort is reflected in the fact that in November, 1992, the Insurance Journal, *a California insurance periodical, named Triwest as, "Agency of the Year."*

To Paul, Quality Concepts is an ongoing process. Said he, "Productivity needs to improve, because there is a tremendous amount of downward pressure on our average commission income. We need to be more efficient just to survive. Reducing errors, especially in today's economic climate, is vital. Our vision is that five years from now, I expect the company will be twice as large; and to do that, we need supervisory or secondary managers that are trained and accountable for their results." Paul concluded by saying, "The quality process we are involved in not only gives us the tools to create a strong leadership base, but also shows us how to work towards our common goals, every day in every way."

THE GOLDEN RULE

What is the secret of leading people successfully? It's no secret, actually. Prophets and philosophers have talked and written about it for thousands of years. It's the Golden Rule: "Do unto others as you would have others do unto you." The golden rule appears in a number of the world's great religions and philosophies. Confucius wrote, "What you do not want done to yourself, do not do to others."

If the golden rule is so important and enjoys such widespread popularity, why don't more people practice it? One reason is that most people don't realize its importance. Another is that it takes tremendous self-control. Most of us are so concerned about how *we* think and feel, that we don't pay nearly enough attention to the thoughts and feelings of others. Self-interest comes naturally; we're all concerned about our own image and our own desires. We don't appreciate that those who work for us are equally concerned about their image and their desires.

And if we don't know how other people think and feel, and we don't make a real effort to find out, how can we possibly put ourselves in their shoes?

In the fall of 1990, Mr. Robert S. K. Tucker, chief executive officer of a large South African corporation, gave a talk in Pretoria, which he titled, *Morality in the Market Place*. In it, Mr. Tucker challenged current business methods which concentrate on bottom-line profits at the expense of society. He refers to one of the dictionary definitions of profit, as, "to be of service, benefit."

Furthermore, he believes that relationships within the corporation are important for its survival. In an interview, Tucker said, "...we aren't in competition with our labor force in order to see whether we can beat them down to the lowest salary level for the highest input of their labor. We are essentially in ... partnership with them. They are a key resource and component..."

He believes that an approach to business which recognizes the needs of the community will result in saving lives, in greater opportunities for third world countries, and less ecological damage to the planet. In fact, he sees a growing awareness of this attitude all over the world, especially in the red-hot debates going on in some business schools.

Practicing what he preaches, Mr. Tucker, whose company is in the field of home financing, made loans to 60,000 black families within five years, whereas previously no such loans had ever been made. His opponents predicted that this would be disastrous, but in fact, the company's profits improved and continue to do so.

DECISION MAKING

What do managers do? They solve problems that arise. They fight fires. They use information and they think. They communicate their ideas to others. They plan for the future and they make decisions. We might say that's really all managers do; that's the purpose of management. Therefore, the best managers are those people who make the best decisions. There are differing styles, or habits, of decision-making. When studied, two major elements generally emerge: the amount of information used and solution focus, one versus many. Some managers use little information before making a decision, and usually do it quickly; others spend more time at it, get input from one or more sources before deciding.

There's nothing wrong with differing styles of decision making. If we all used the same style, the result would be "group think," which might be dangerous, to say nothing of boring. However, to be effective leaders, we need to recognize our style and that of others. Here at Quality Concepts, many of our clients use The Driver Dynamic Decision Styles method with excellent results.

Some years ago, when Mike Perrault, president of Advanced Teamware Publishing, Inc., and a Quality Concepts colleague, was training military officers, he discovered that all flight instructors—without exception—made decisions authoritatively. When he pointed this out, his students laughed and said, "That's called natural selection. We're the only ones left alive."

I understand that. If I'm in an airplane and the pilot has to make a quick decision, I'd rather the pilot be someone who's used to making decisions quickly and with minimum information. On the other hand, I want the designers of that airplane to seek plenty of information beforehand, and do a lot of studying before they finalize their design.

Because the fact is, the more information that is available and studied and used, the better the decision-making. It's rare that an autocratic decision will be the very best; although, as in the case of a pilot with a life-or-death proposition, speed may occasionally be more important than consultation. That's where experience comes in handy, since experience is an accumulation of information.

The Japanese boast that their employees don't use only their hands; they use their brains too. Toyota receives over a million suggestions a year from employees, and 97 percent of them are used in some way! In addition, the Japanese encourage input from workers before decisions are made. They invented quality circles so that the best ideas of all members could be applied to finding solutions to problems. Even when American businesses began to apply this concept, they found that the Japanese spent far more time at it than we did. They didn't even begin to discuss the problem itself until they had established the *rules* for discussing it. What criteria shall we use? What process?

When a group sits down to discuss a problem and come up with a solution, what happens if some disagree with the result? In a democracy, we're used to the concept that the majority rules. There are winners and losers. But if a business is to run smoothly, you can't afford to have losers, who may resent the fact that their side didn't win, who will be less than enthusiastic about implementing the group solution, who may in fact, actually try to sabotage the method in an effort to show that *their* idea should have been followed instead.

The Japanese use a consensus method. They try to get everyone to agree on the best course of action. This is similar to our judicial system, in which a jury is required to agree on the verdict. Some of the jurors might have reservations, but they feel they can support the others' decision.

In looking for consensus in finding solutions, managers need to hold meetings that promote cooperation and exchange information, not to issue orders dictatorially. While we generally don't encourage more meetings, there's a difference between wasting time and gathering information that will prevent

doing it over!

It's also a good idea to get rid of the rectangular conference table. At a typical conference, the boss sits at the head of the table and talks to a few people close to him. Those along the sides, especially those near the opposite end, can barely *see* the others at the table, much less hear or participate. The Round Table is as good an idea for management meetings, as it was for knights of old; but an oval one may be as close as we can come to it today.

Try not to put employees in positions where they compete with one another. Don't have contests that pit one group against another. Instead, set up goals for everyone to meet. Write down the rules on an easel pad or flip chart as a public record for all to see and agree upon. Try for a win-win situation.

IDENTIFYING YOUR STYLE

Within these two basic management styles: autocratic and democratic (for lack of a better word) there are further breakdowns possible. For instance, an autocratic manager may quickly focus on one solution. We might describe this person as action-oriented, decisive, spontaneous, reliable, efficient. But another may be open to the possibility of other solutions. This person is described as adaptable, open, flexible, in favor of variety. Another manager, who prefers to get a considerable amount of information before making a decision may also come up with what he or she feels is the only right solution; that person could be called analytical, methodical, logical, thorough, persistent. Whereas another may explore many possibilities and thereby earn the description of creative, exploratory, a listener, even "laid-back."

No one, however, is only one type of decision-maker at all times. We tend to be mixtures of these styles, although most of us have a dominant "go to" style we use in our comfort zone and yet another when our environmental load gets too high. Furthermore, we may have one style that we use frequently, which is our public image (a "role" style), and quite another that we actually use when we're not aware of others (a "natural" style).

What's the value of knowing this much about ourselves? To the extent that we need to make our short time on earth as pleasant as possible, understanding ourselves can be an end in itself. When it comes to managing a corporation, it's vitally important to know how we make decisions, so that we can alter our style as necessary. We have to get along with others; and in order to lead them, we must first know ourselves. Understanding these various styles—deciding which of them our fellow managers use—can make our jobs easier and our commitment to quality a more reasonable goal.

A manager can't do everything, no matter what the job description says. So, if you know yourself, you can delegate certain tasks to those staff members whose style is appropriate; and you can avoid conflicts by recognizing that all styles are right and necessary somewhere, some time. You can also develop people who can do your job. That frees you to revisit your vision and your team players and to take on additional responsibility.

In *When Smart People Fail* (Simon & Schuster, 1987), Hyatt and Gottlieb point out that the average middle manager spends 38 percent of his time in meetings. Senior management spends 53 percent of its time in meetings. Unless you know your management style and that of your fellow managers, at least one-third of this time is wasted, because you cannot come up with good decisions, decisions that will reveal errors, rearrange priorities and result in success. Over 90 percent of the executive recruitments that don't work out, and are chalked up to "bad chemistry," turn out to have been the result of inadequate understanding of decision-making styles.

Hundreds of years ago, China's Sun Tzu wrote about the value of knowing yourself and your enemy in *The Art of War*. By substituting the word "competition" for "enemy," I've updated this age-old wisdom to apply to business. "If you know the competition and know yourself, you need not fear the result of a hundred battles. If you know yourself but not the competition, for every victory gained you will also suffer a defeat. If you know neither the competition nor yourself, you might as well FAX in your resignation."

MANAGEMENT SKILLS

During World War II, a lot of people went through officers' training school. After the war, they applied the leadership methods they had learned to their business experience; and the many studies done about management determined that there were three main skills: technical, human, and systems.

Technical skills are those involved with the job at hand: how to run the machine, put things together, make the blivet. Human skills deal with people, our customers, fellow-workers and suppliers. Systems skills are those involved in running the organization: getting orders, finding suppliers, setting up budgets, etc. By far the most important of these skills are the human ones. In his book, *Becoming a Leader*, Warren Bennis points out that the single biggest reason for failing in business is "not getting along with people." Next comes incompatibility with the job or the people; and finally incompatibility with the values of the company.

In his time, John D. Rockefeller was the richest man in America. He said, "The ability to deal with people is as purchasable a commodity as sugar and coffee. And *I will pay more for that ability than for any other under the sun!*"

Back in 1921 when $50 a week was considered a good salary, Charles M. Schwab (not Charles R. Schwab, who started the discount brokerage firm of the same name) was hired as president of U.S. Steel at $3,000 a day! Why? Was he a genius? Did he know more about steel than anyone else? No. Schwab admitted he had people working for him who knew more about making steel than he did. He was paid more than a million dollars a year *for his ability to deal with people.*

One of America's leading engineering colleges admits that only 15 percent of an engineer's financial success is due to technical knowledge, while 85 percent is due to *skill in human engineering,* the ability to lead and deal with people.

Since this is the highest priced ability under the sun, wouldn't you suppose every college in the land would offer courses in it? If you hear of one, let us know.

This is the golden age of technology. Of every $40 spent on research in American businesses in recent years, $38.50 went to improving technical skills, only $1.50 to improving human skills. In the '30's and '40's, visions of the twenty-first century often showed everything being done by robots instead of people. Yet, as we approach that date, we find exactly the opposite is true. The more sophisticated our machines, the more we depend on the expertise of the people running them. In addition, Dr. Joyce Brothers, reporting on a study which kept track of workmen's compensation claims, found that the biggest single reason for claims now—25 percent—is for stress, a psychological rather than physical disorder. Why are we ignoring the mental and emotional health of our workers, when studies often show that happy, knowledgeable employees lead to satisfied customers, which leads to success?

KICK ROCKS, NOT BUTT

Ray Kroc, who made McDonald's into the giant it is today, once said, "I believe that if you hire a man to do a job, you ought to get out of the way and let him do it. If you doubt his ability, you shouldn't have hired him in the first place."

I subscribe to the idea that management's job is to define the purpose and goals of the company very clearly, then spend the rest of their time smoothing the path, kicking rocks out of the way, and generally making it as easy as possible for the company (i.e., the employees) to move toward the objective. Top management defines the goals, of course, but all levels of management should kick rocks.

Too often, however, management spends more time placing obstacles in the path of progress than in removing them. Peter Drucker says, "Most of what we call management consists of making it difficult for people to get their work done." This takes the form of needless restrictions, suppression of ideas, invention of endless paperwork, organizational shuffling, performance reports, and petty controls of various kinds, which swamp employees' productive capacity, and destroy morale. The real leaders in any organization are the ones who kick the most rocks out of the way of progress.

When I worked for A-M in San Jose, California, one of my clients was Hewlett-Packard. Behind every manager's desk was a sign with the letters "MBWA." I asked about it and was told the letters stood for "Management By Wandering Around." This was in 1969, when Tom Peters was still in school; later Peters used the phrase, "management by walking around." At Hewlett-Packard, a fine company, managers were encouraged to go through the plant and find out what the employees were thinking and doing. It was how they kept in touch with the real problems of production and were better able to kick rocks out of the way so that progress could take place.

Writing in *Business Month* Magazine, Daniel M. Kehrer describes the management style of Harry V. Quadracci, founder and president of Quad/Graphics, Inc. "...he sees how far he can back away from control—by shifting it to other people... It's control hooked to freedom. It relies heavily on trust.

"While many CEO's have adopted the 'management by walking around' approach, Harry Quadracci seems to manage more by walking away. He lets people manage themselves and, through that responsibility, achieve things they never thought themselves capable of achieving... (this) brand of management... has proved to be a major morale booster for the employees and problems have been few."

What Quadracci seems to be saying is that if you give employees a feeling that they're responsible for doing a good job and that you trust them enough to let them do it, they won't take advantage of you. Every year, since 1974, he holds a "Spring Fling," a day when management plays hooky, leaving the rank and file in charge of the company. Yet, with no one watching, the employees continue to do their jobs, as well as on any other day, and take pride in their accomplishment.

Although Quad/Graphics is technology based, the firm does not have thousands of engineers. The average employee is only a high-school graduate. Yet the loose style of management there does not mean they have low standards. All the employees are treated as if they are engineers and they respond by working each day to prove they're worthy and able to learn and improve on the job. As a result, Quad/Graphics has grown at a rate of 40 percent a year and become one of America's largest printing companies.

CHANGE FOR GROWTH

In order to grow, a company must make changes. Think of the entrepreneur as someone who, with an idea and resources, starts a company. This start-up is like driving a rocket ship into orbit. Fuel is burned (people are employed), and, once sufficient energy is created, lift-off begins. During this mode, usually only one person can be in charge; that person must make every decision, whether it's buying equipment or hiring. The leader creates an almost cult-like environment, such as the one Apple put together to develop the Macintosh. People come to work early, they work hard, and they stay late. Fuel.

As this rocket—or business—rises in the community, it attracts competition, which may be likened to gravity, trying to hold back its rise, but eventually, with enough of the "Right Stuff," it reaches a relatively stable platform, somewhat like a space station. At this juncture the leader must recognize a paradigm shift takes place: going from the ascent mode to staying in its orbit.

This transition is difficult and we could not begin to list the number of companies whose rocket has flamed-out prematurely and augured into the ground. And rarely will you find an individual who is capable of leading and managing both the rocket mode and the stable-orbit mode. Bill Gates of Microsoft seems to be one who does. He is technically strong and understands the people side of business. The antithesis would be Steven Jobs of Apple who was finally booted out by the board of directors, as his entrepreneuring ways would not allow him to make the transition necessary for long-term growth. Jobs left and promptly began to build another rocket. As leaders, we must first know our strengths and stick with what we do best.

Any analogy can only be carried so far. Unlike a rocket, which, when it has reached its destination, is no longer needed (at least for the time being), a business must continue to function, albeit differently. This transition is a major crossroads for the continuation of the company; but these changes need not exclude the caring concern of its founders. Although some owner/developers may lack the vision and long-term strategies necessary to build the stages that will turn a small company into a multinational giant, the reason for its initial development—the "mission statement" if you will—should remain a vital part of the transition process. After the first stage has passed, new managers, with the skill and resources to keep the company moving ahead, may be needed.

Only a relatively few individuals may be capable of stepping gracefully away from what they have created and seek help from outside. It's heart-wrenching to leave a group of people who shared their blood, sweat and tears in the beginning, or to recognize that some of them won't be able to function properly in the new mode. Sam Walton is an example of one who did recognize the need to step back; he became Chairman Emeritus or Designated Store Visitor, and wouldn't we all like to have *his* success?

A simple case of "doing the right thing" comes from Coast Index Company. Harry Ruotsala, the president and founder, recognized an individual who, in the beginning, gave her all, and yet, with the company's growth and evolution to more sophisticated tasks, was not capable of performing to the level necessary to keep up with others. Harry took it upon himself to find a job for this person where she could perform, be recognized for that performance and gain, not only a continued salary, but the gift of psychic income as a part of the company that she had helped build.

Unfortunately, this is only one small success story. Many organizations will not, cannot, bring themselves to make these difficult decisions. But loyal workers can often be retrained, rather than discarded; if not, their role in the expanding company must be examined. Whether by retraining former workers or hiring from without, managers must still be committed to quality, values and integrity. If they lack leadership and an understanding of people, they may inadvertently give rise to an onboard terrorist who, in the beginning, had nothing but the very best intentions, but ultimately hurt the organization.

Failure to heed these lessons can be unpleasant at best. An entrepreneur I know, who started his business from his kitchen with a few neighbors, while diapered children ran around the house, watched it grow into a multi-office company beyond the owner's wildest dreams. But expansion brought troubles with bank loans, suppliers and original employees who felt left behind and caused problems. Eventually the bank appointed one of their executives to put the company in order and the founder was relegated to a corner office with the title Product Innovator, and virtually no say in the running of his business.

While living in Iowa, I attended a Lutheran church which began with twelve founding families and a young pastor. The church grew and attracted many new families; but after three years, the pastor was removed and sent to another parish. When we protested, he explained to us that a founding pastor can become too close to the original families who worked so hard to sustain the church. As new members come in, an attitude of new versus old, or "we versus them" can prevail. But a new pastor has no such loyalties and can bring all church members together in harmony. Many corporations could learn how to build for success by taking a page out of this church building manual.

MANAGING IN TOUGH TIMES

In 1989, after seven years of growth, the U.S. began to suffer a downturn. These business cycles happen all the time, but some are more severe than others. The true test of management occurs during these down periods. How do *you* react? Do you, like some managers, decide to fire all the sales people until business gets better? That's a sure way to sabotage yourself.

Sure, expenses need to be cut during slumping sales, but eliminating the sales staff isn't the way to go about it. During depressed periods of Toyota's existence, workers were taken off the line, given blue jackets and sent door to door throughout Japan to sell automobiles.

When IBM was faced with the same problem, they didn't fire the sales people. On the contrary, they transferred *everybody* to sales. Every person, whether engineer, secretary or repairman, was encouraged to look for business and *sell* IBM as the company that could fill their needs.   In *The Father, the Son and the Company*, (Bantam Books, 1990), Thomas J. Watson, Jr. tells how his father hired sales people in down periods, even though his contemporaries snickered behind his back. At this writing, IBM is again suffering through difficult times. According to *Computer Wars*, by Charles Ferguson and Charles Morris, Big Blue, which once epitomized America's global technological dominance, suffered huge losses because, the authors point out, "company politics evolved into a 'cult of personality' style of leadership that resisted new ideas..." It's my feeling, however, that IBM will prevail due to Watson Sr.'s sound basic philosophy of customer service.

There are plenty of ways you can keep your company from floundering if you keep your lights turned on. Yes, you should reduce waste wherever you find it, cut unnecessary spending, perhaps eliminate ineffective employees. But the positive steps are far more important: look for new ideas and techniques, study your customers' businesses and see if you can provide more services for them, ask for referrals, listen to your employees. It all starts with you, the leader. That's why you're paid more than your workers: not just to supervise them, but to take the initiative in providing ways to make the company grow.

Challenge: What will you do to improve management skills, kick rocks out of the way, and make change for growth?

_____

_____

_____

_____

_____

8

LEADERSHIP

You can manage things; you must lead people.
Wilma Vaught, Brig. Gen., USAF Ret.

NEEDED: MBL's, NOT MBA's

When I started Quality Concepts, my goal was to train employees how to do quality work for both internal and external customers. I persuaded two friends to let me practice on their companies; and, ten minutes into my first presentation, I got the lucky break that showed me the key element. A woman stood up and asked, "Have you told this to *them* yet?" *Them* was management and I was reminded that management commitment must come first.

Michael Perrault, previously mentioned, is an expert in the fields of management decision making and organizational behavior. He has worked with such firms as Aerojet, Eli Lilly, McDonald Douglas, Syntex, United Parcel Service, Union Bank and Xerox, among others. In his opinion American businesses are over-managed and under-led!

MBA means Master of Business Administration; yet MBA whiz-kids, fresh from prestigious universities, have been allowed to acquire, merge, downsize and restructure American companies. The result is more often than not, they've been fed into the waiting jaws of foreign competition. What is needed is not more MBA's, but a few MBL's, Masters of Business Leadership.

While looking for quality as the savior of American business in the '90's, these spreadsheet worshipers see only the numbers and statistics. They are impersonal. But, as Tom Peters so clearly spelled out in *A Passion for Excellence* (Random House, 1985), passionate leadership is required for the achievement of true quality and survival. Passion is an emotion, and true leadership is emotional too. It's caring tremendously about creating a quality company and translating that caring into appropriate methods: sometimes strong, sometimes compassionate, but always toward a positive goal.

Real leaders don't fool themselves and others into thinking they have all the answers. Moreover, they're courageous enough to admit it. They know their strengths and weaknesses, and seek to surround themselves with others who complement their abilities. They're humble enough to ask questions when necessary and search for answers in unusual places. They know that decisions often involve risk-taking; and, when some decisions don't work out, they accept this fact of life and go forward without recriminations, trying to learn from the experience so that particular mistake won't be repeated.

True leaders must delegate authority and thereby develop other leaders for the future prosperity of the company. They recognize responsibility for motivating others, and don't assign blame for underachieving if the environment didn't provide the means and opportunity to achieve.

Leaders have a mission, or goal, in mind at all times and they submit this to their workers at every level. They must be open to feedback from employees, to learn if they understand these goals and how to achieve them. Leaders develop teamwork, trust, and a sense of belonging; and they inspire people to excel.

Warren Bennis, professor at the University of Southern California School of Business, says: "American... captains of industry have never been more celebrated and less effective."

He sees the rush to get an MBA ironic in a time when competitors are beating us at every turn; and he blames this in part on the fact that companies which used to be led by their owner/developer, who cared deeply about his company, his workers and his community, are now managed by professional wheeler-dealers whose only concern is the appearance of progress while actually looking forward to moving on to their next golden parachute.

Tom Flood, executive vice president of Capital Bank in Miami, says there are five traits that a good leader must have:

1. A spirit of initiative: Seeing the need to do something and then actually doing it.
2. Ability to take a risk: The willingness to do something different, or to change from past experiences.
3. A sense of responsibility: Making decisions and then accepting the outcome.
4. Authenticity: Personal characteristics, such as integrity, honesty, trustworthiness, reliability.
5. Generosity: Being generous, not with money, but with the most valuable of things, your time; to look outward rather than being totally self-focused.

"The Masters Business program," Tom says, "is only now beginning to add leadership to the curriculum. Before that, leadership was never dealt with. The only people I ever found who had leadership training were those who got it in military service. Through Bob's Total Quality Leadership sessions, I know that Capital Bank's 200 managers are going to be exposed to leadership training, and if they have my 'famous five' traits, they'll recognize that it's their responsibility to put what they learn into practice and create an environment where business can thrive."

BAD BOSSES

In the lexicon of the street, "bad" means good as in, "He's a baaaad dude, man." Even in business, for awhile it seemed as if "bad" in its traditional sense was indeed the way to a privileged life. But the tide is turning. The end of the '80's saw one after another of these "bad dudes" falling: Ivan Boesky, Mike Milken, Jim Bakker, Leona Helmsley, Charles Keating. To succeed in the '90's you have to wake up to the fact that excess is out and old-fashioned integrity and ethics are in.

One of the managing styles we need to eliminate is what I call "ice hockey management." Ten guys get sticks, somebody drops a puck, and they beat each other to death. The CEO drops the puck, which is an idea. The rest of them worry about budgets, their backs, and their BMW payments. And nobody gets the puck toward the goal. It often takes a significant event to wake up management to the necessity for doing more than just dropping the puck.

In this age, leaders must encourage—no, *insist*—that employees bring their energy and brains to the job, to determine ways to continually reduce errors and increase productivity. It's counterproductive to stifle creative thinking. Standards which may be achievable by some, could be doubled or tripled by other employees.

At the same time, it's important to clearly distinguish between jobs which require strict adherence to standards or directions and those which encourage people to stretch and exceed standards, adding to the growth, profit and excellence of the organization. The responsibility clearly rests with leaders to determine the function of each position and be certain each employee understands whether the job calls for strict adherence to a measurable standard, or can benefit from creative thinking. Additionally, employees must be told how they're doing, specifically and immediately, either with positive reinforcement or corrective information.

Executives of the '90's must instill trust into the troops. They can't speak one way and act another (you gotta walk what you talk). They must develop loyalty to the company because high-performing employees are going to be harder to find and keep.

Loyal workers don't take kindly to displays of privilege and perks that aren't applicable to them, like close-in parking places, executive washrooms and use of the company yacht.

CEO's may *say* they want teamwork, but, when employees see that there are different offices and dress codes, separate dining rooms, time clocks versus discretionary hours, and wildly different fringe benefits, they quickly get the message that some team members are more equal than others.

Unfortunately, the adversarial approach is far from dead in corporate America. What else but a "we" versus "them" attitude accounts for the fact that while some companies are beginning to implement a pay scale for workers based on how much they exceed their quotas, their top officers continue to increase their own salaries regardless of the fortunes of the companies they head? While such programs force blue-collar employees to share the risk that goes with business, the boss seems to be immune.

American CEO salaries have been increasing faster than revenues and profits for many years, while European, Canadian and Japanese executives make less than half as much. Although employees may not strike over their bosses making 160 times more than they do, some shareholders are beginning to question such practices. When the company's earnings decline, why should its chief executive officer receive a pay raise?

As the baby-bust of the '70's and '80's brings fewer and fewer workers into the job force in the '90's and beyond, greed and status symbols at the top of the corporate ladder will not go unnoticed; and quality employees will gravitate toward companies where the disparity between compensation of one group over another is not so blatant and discriminatory.

Fortunately, a few heads of corporations and their boards of directors are setting compensation guidelines that are more in line with reality. More and more leaders are walking through the plants and learning names, or eating in the cafeteria with everybody else. And we've seen some company parking lots where the close-in spaces are reserved for people who get there first.

Visit Zumar Industries, in City of Commerce, California, where large metal stars are affixed to posts in front of the closest parking spaces and reserved for the "Star of the Quarter," or, "Star of the Year." When Raul Huerra, who works in the die cutting department, won the Star of the Quarter award, his eyes lit up and he said he felt truly honored to be recognized, even though, at that time, he didn't own a car to park in it. (He has since acquired one.) Roger Milliken, CEO of Milliken Textiles, insists on parking in the furthest possible space from the building so he can walk through the parking lot, speak to employees, see what they're driving, and get a better sense of his people.

Forward-looking executives will get quality production when they unlearn abusive treatment of employees. They can no longer rule by intimidation, criticism or humiliation. No one can do productive work, much less high-quality work, when shadowed by fear. anxiety or the whip of disdain.

We're all familiar with the story of *The Mutiny on the Bounty* and Captain Bligh, who was not fictitious, but a real English naval officer. It was the custom in the 18th century to treat sailors more like cattle than human beings. Not surprisingly, few men signed on for English ships. If men were needed, the officers sent thugs into bars where they hit someone over the head and he woke up the next morning on the high seas, probably chained. There were no arguments on that ship, because if you talked back, you were flogged or keel-hauled. Bligh was one of the worst examples of that type of officer; even his second-in-command, Fletcher Christian, could finally stand it no longer, and the result was the famous mutiny.

Are there still some companies with Captain Bligh types as managers? If you're an employee and have a problem and you go to Mister Bligh, what does he say to you? "What's the matter with you? How long have you been here? I gave you the answer to that last week. Get out of here!" So you go back to your job and you make your best guess and pray that it's right. And everyone else in the immediate vicinity learns the lesson too: don't go to Bligh for help because he won't give it to you. And lots of work gets done wrong (Remember, employees never forget.) and then we get to

do it over again.

In other companies, the good leader, the coach, hangs up the phone, or stops what she's doing and goes to help. She says, "I'm glad you asked that. There's no such thing as a dumb question." Now I know this is not easy to do when you've got three fires burning, four balls in the air, and time is short. But, while change is difficult, it's extremely rewarding. The good coach may be thinking, "This is the most incredibly stupid kid I've ever seen," but she doesn't say that aloud. She brightens up and answers the question. Later, she'll see that the young man gets more training, but right now she knows that this job has to be ready by noon on Saturday and there isn't time to do it over again. Which is what will happen if the guy is allowed to do it wrong.

Or she gets someone else to help with the problem. And she makes the employees feel good, instead of scared. We like that kind of leader; we'll go to great lengths for her. Setting him adrift in a boat was too good for Captain Bligh.

The enlightened executive develops teamwork among the employees. Rather than talking down to them, she asks their opinions, takes their suggestions seriously, and makes them feel valued and important. She creates an atmosphere in which workers feel free to voice their concerns and in which they can take responsibility and practice self-supervision.

The '90's executives won't just fire people. Their vision and innate ability to attract associates and markets will assure growth and the creation of more jobs. Moreover, if some employees turn out to be real On-Board Terrorists, the team will throw them off the boat!

INFORMATION IS POWER

If you would lead people effectively today you have to let them know what's going on. Employees can't work efficiently or enthusiastically in a vacuum. Some bosses make a practice of holding back information, telling people only the minimum facts they need to handle their jobs. That's a serious mistake. Whether or not something directly affects people, or is in their area of responsibility is beside the point. You can't stop people from thinking and wondering. Ignorance of the facts causes gossiping, misunderstandings and needless resentment.

A great many organizations—and bosses—are unnecessarily secretive. Their attitude is that if employees don't have to know something, don't tell them. They figure it's none of their business. But employees continue to speculate about things. As a result, the organization becomes a hotbed of rumors. All bad.

The smartest policy is to tell employees *everything* you possibly can, give them all the information they might be interested in. Keep them so well supplied with correct information that rumors don't have a chance to get a foothold.

Think carefully before trying to keep anything secret. Be sure it's absolutely necessary. Secrets rarely keep for long, anyway, and they breed distrust when they're eventually discovered or revealed. Once a decision is made about anything, the wisest course is to announce it as fast as you can, before the grapevine beats you to it.

One of the common barriers between managers and employees is a lack of trust; the feeling that the person on top isn't being on the level, that management is keeping a card or two up its sleeve. If you act secretively, this feeling is intensified. Everyone likes to be in on things. They like their supervisors to take them into their confidence and keep them fully informed. When they don't, the employees don't feel very important, or very enthusiastic about cooperating.

In a recent survey of what managers and workers think of ten different aspects of the work environment, the disparity between them was glaringly apparent. Where managers thought "good wages" was first on employees' lists, it was actually fifth. What really came in first on employees' lists was "Appreciation for good work," yet managers rated it as eighth out of ten. And where managers thought "Feeling 'in' on things" would rank tenth, the employees themselves rated it second!

Good bosses try to keep their people fully informed at all times. They think it's an important part of their jobs, they take it seriously and try to do it well. They know that when information stops, negative rumors start. They want cooperation, not just compliance; keeping people well informed, promptly, is essential to getting it. And it costs practically nothing.

QUALITY LEADERSHIP

The components of quality leadership are threefold:

1. A clear, concrete message that conveys a particular strategy which people can begin to act on.
2. Demonstration by the leaders' behavior that they intend to enforce and reward quality-oriented actions.

3. An energetic follow-through process in which management takes action to provide the necessary training and resources and to align the systems and procedures of the organization so as to make them support the new quality philosophy and strategy.

QUALITY ROLLS DOWNHILL

One of the things we learn after we get some wrinkles and grey hair is that quality starts at the top and goes downhill. That's why Leadership, and not just Management, is so important. In order to lead people effectively, we need to understand how to apply quality to their jobs. It's been proved many times that—all other things being equal—people remember 10 percent of what they hear, 20 percent of what they see, 50 percent of what they read, and 90 percent of what they actually do. Therefore, a leader must not only *tell* employees what he wants them to do, he must engage them in the actual practice of it; otherwise it doesn't get recorded on the disk in their multi-billion dollar device.

Adults learn best under specific circumstances, and the greatest learning occurs when they take responsibility. In other words, my attitude must not be, "It's his responsibility to teach me whether I want to learn or not," but rather, "It's my responsibility to learn, whether he's a great teacher or not." Therefore, an effective leader must motivate people to accept this responsibility. Adults also learn most effectively when they understand that it's personally beneficial. This means a leader must point out those benefits: such as, doing this right creates a satisfied customer, brings a pay bonus, or prestige among peers, or a promotion in the future.

Adults also learn when they discover things for themselves. It's always better, not to *tell* an employee why something doesn't work right, but to ask a series of questions that allows him to discover it for himself.

Finally, they learn more from experience and feedback, than from experience alone. When a new experience comes along, you think about it, you study it, you note what new information goes along with it, you develop a new course of action based on it, and finally you apply the new course.

Two similar names come to mind. Michael Milken, who once earned $500 million a year with Drexel, Burnham, Lambert, went to prison. Roger Milliken, of Milliken & Company, is considered by many people the country's best CEO.

John Hillkirk, writing in *U.S.A. Today*, says, "You'd never know that he runs the show at this textile giant, which took in an estimated $2.9 billion in 1989 revenue. Milliken's magic is rooted in the philosophy that nobody is better than anybody else. At Milliken, no one has a private office. All 14,300 employees are referred to as associates. No one except the Associate of the Month gets a reserved parking place. 'The secret is in asking workers what they think and showing them that you really care,' Milliken says."

Milliken's plants won five of the ten excellence awards given by General Motors in 1988 to its 5,000 U.S. suppliers. Milliken won the Malcolm Baldrige National Quality Award in 1989. Presenting the award, President Bush called the company's leadership style "sheer 21st century."

In the past, Milliken & Co. operated like many American companies. Management ruled with complete authority. Then, Roger Milliken began to realize that labor was not responsible for poor quality, management was. He also understood that the very survival of his company was at stake.

Now, signs of those changes are everywhere. Bulletin boards report the number of error-free days they've achieved; employees are encouraged to submit improvement ideas and supervisors must acknowledge them within 72 hours. Now called an associate, the average worker submitted 20 suggestions last year and 85 percent were implemented. They're empowered to find problems and then solve them. Unlike Japanese workers, Americans need individual recognition, so a party is held each time someone gets 20 ideas accepted.

"Perhaps the biggest change has been psychological," Hillkirk reports, "convincing hourly people that nothing is more important than what they think and how they feel. To change attitudes, employees' achievements must be tracked closely and rewarded every step of the way. The hard-driving Milliken president, Thomas Malone, a former college football player, puts it this way: 'I broke my nose five times, lost one-third of my teeth in football; do you think I'd do all that if there were no fans in the crowd and no scoreboard at the end of the field?'"

TEAMWORK

John Toal, President of Toal & Associates Advertising, says TEAM is an acronym that means Together Everyone Accomplishes More. That's a great definition. Companies that are succeeding today are those that instill a teamwork spirit.

When we first began studying the Japanese system to learn why they turned out products that were both better and cheaper, our initial focus was on improving the quality of the product itself: finding defects and eliminating them, finding faster and cheaper methods to build the blivets. It was only later that we realized that was not the *means*, but the *result* of their methods. In actuality, they built teams first and then the quality products followed.

Another thing we noticed about the Japanese was their company song and uniforms. I don't know of any American firms that have songs, but plenty of them require their employees to wear uniforms. A well-known real estate firm gives bright-colored blazers to its sales people; certain banks have done the same for tellers and managers on the banking floor. Even public schools are finding that students who wear school uniforms behave better and there is a dramatic drop in school yard violence.

One of the tasks confronting leaders is to convince their employees the company uniform is important. Even if you don't have a uniform per se, the corporate world does have a dress code. When some employees refuse to conform, the leader can use teamwork to correct the situation, reminding the employee that teams have uniforms, and a basketball player would no more refuse to wear his uniform than he would refrain from making the tie-breaking basket. Imagine the NFL, NBA, NHA or baseball without uniforms. What draws many players is the desire to wear the team colors.

Leaders require people skills, and, like a baseball player who fails to cooperate or shows poor sportsmanship and thus gets kicked off the team, employees must learn that teamwork is the key to keeping their jobs. Football players who follow instructions become "most valuable players" and get fat contracts; in industry, too, rewards go to the team members who support the company's goals and priorities.

The "kinder, gentler" nation that George Bush invited us to build when he was President, is part and parcel of the team spirit that can, incidentally, create more efficient and profitable companies. Every time Nordstrom is mentioned as a company that is succeeding because of its team attitude, a few naysayers speak up with, "Yeah, just wait until the economy turns down and then see what happens to Nordstrom." The fact is, if we all work to create better teamwork, production will go up, forestalling or minimizing an economic downturn. Our quality products would become more marketable, not only within the United States, but abroad.

We need leaders who have vision, a long-term approach that respects others, not managers whose philosophy is "work 'em or shoot 'em." We've had plenty of those in the past. Failed companies were filled with managers with this mentality. It left the company panting for breath, paying an extraordinarily high price for the coming and going of employees and, ultimately, with customer dissatisfaction.

Teamwork leads to success. An idea may come from one person, but the team may be necessary to bring that idea to fruition. The employee can end up frustrated, fatigued and disappointed instead of accomplishing the job swiftly and correctly and being left with a sense of accomplishment.

Take a simple example of trying to move a large box across a room. If one person does it, he may find there are unlimited possibilities for disaster. First, the box may break and the contents spill out, possibly ruining them. Second—even worse—he experiences a strange sensation in his back and can't straighten up.

That's an obvious example. What's not so obvious are the times we have a mental problem to solve, rather than a physical one and yet we fail to ask for help because we're embarrassed to admit we need it. Look at the positive results though: the person you asked for assistance is complimented that you asked for his help. You've created an atmosphere for synergism: that is the force created when people work together that is greater than the sum of its parts. Not only did the job get done; we feel good when we win together. We've created camaraderie and increased our psychic income.

A successful football team—or any other team—can't work effectively if everyone speaks a different language. For a while the Buffalo Bills had great players, but a poor team. In 1987 they turned that completely around. (They've been in the playoffs since then.) The coach, Marv Levy, visited the team members during the off season. He met their families and became aware of their various personalities. He let the players' wives and children know that he cared. A team that works together has it all over one with brilliant individual players who bump into each other on the field.

Some managers don't believe in company picnics and similar activities, because of the cost and because not everyone shows up. But it's not about eating or attendance; it's about creating opportunities for team building. If employees play softball and volleyball, those who don't show up will realize what they missed during the Monday morning conversations, and they'll show up next year. As the team begins to gel, those who don't care (possible O.B.T.s) will spin off and go away. They can't stand teamwork and the excitement of quality work and winning, perhaps because they're afraid to try.

One of the best group activities I ever saw occurred among employees of a bank. Alan Bredeson, Vice President and General Manager of Security Pacific merchant card services, held a sales meeting every six months; but on this occasion he held it at a resort in Palm Springs. On the final afternoon, a local firm who specializes in this type of activity, put on a "Mini-Olympics." The group was divided into three teams, each with its own colored tee-shirts; and they participated in a series of events —some athletic, some intellectual, some simply hysterical—staged by "referees" in striped shirts. There was music, and both still pictures and videotapes of everything. At the dinner party that night well over half the people received awards, not just for winning games, but for "the slowest," "most enthusiastic," and "most original" (for the team songs, slogans or skits). Trophies still sit on winners' desks, and the event is still talked about. It helped build a team that worked together so well they went on to accomplish a very difficult system change in record time.

The leadership style that is truly concerned about *all* the employees, in *every* job in the company, will create a team that produces quality products and long-term customer satisfaction. You win, they win, the customers win, and profits are a natural byproduct of the effort.

Create your own champions and heroes. Stop telling Nordstrom stories. Tell your own. Get your competition telling stories about you and then you will find yourself riding on the shoulders of the team you've built. You will have created a legacy that will follow you throughout your career and your life. When the topic is success, you'll be the one they talk about.

INTERVIEW with LUMBER CITY

In 1986, Jess Ruf took over Lumber City. He recognized immediately that drastic methods were required to save this home improvement based business, made up of many retail locations throughout the Southern California market area. Mr. Ruf is a hands on manager and immediately began making the rounds of the stores, visiting with each and every employee. They began calling these sessions "donuts with Jess."

During these visits, he would ask the employees what should be done to make Lumber City a better company. The meetings had a positive effect on morale. Besides inspiring numerous workable suggestions, most importantly it became quickly apparent that Jess Ruf was a man of integrity and honesty, and good people will respond to those values.

In 1987 Ruf hired Quality Concepts to continue the work he had begun. This left Jess free to concentrate on the financial and marketing aspects of his business.

"It took people to ruin the company," Jess says, "and it takes people to turn it around. If they're at the top, the process goes a lot faster. We developed a cultural language, reinforced quality procedures, and indoctrinated both new employees and management level people with the desire to 'do it right the first time' because it was the right thing to do."

It took two years of development, but now there seems to be the right mix of dedicated employees. Quality Concepts' programs such as Solution Selling Skills and Leading and Managing People, strengthened teamwork throughout the organization and galvanized the employees into a well trained, focused and spirited group who are taking Lumber City to new heights in the home improvement industry.

Under Jess Ruf's outstanding vision and leadership, Lumber City (now named "Do-It Center") continues to outperform its competition. Jess's ability to attract, hire and retain high quality employees—providing dedicated people throughout the company—is one of the keys to his success. Jess believes in people and fulfills their needs by training in both people-oriented (creating and retaining relationships) and technical skills. He involves them in decisions and listens to their suggestions.

Do-It Center employees are empowered to "do the right thing" to guarantee customer satisfaction and repeat business. This assures their psychic income as well as a continued paycheck for all. Fielding a championship team is Jess's sustainable competitive advantage.

Challenge: What will you do to improve leadership skills in your organization?

_____

_____

_____

_____

_____

_____

_____

_____

Most successful people are not working for the money. They're working for the rewards...the satisfaction...the challenge of it...to win.

Michael J. Cutino, Publisher, *Nightlife* magazine

COMMUNICATION

Silence gives consent, or a horrible feeling that nobody's listening.

Franklin P. Jones

There's a joke going around in which a peasant sees a wise man (he probably wears a beard, carries a lamp and has a faraway look in his eyes). The peasant asks, "Why is there so much trouble in the world?" And the wise man says, "Wise men don't talk to peasants." The peasant wanders off, muttering, "I thought it was more complicated than that."

THE COMMUNICATION PYRAMID

Any business is made up of three factors: the management its employees and its customers. Together they form a pyramid.

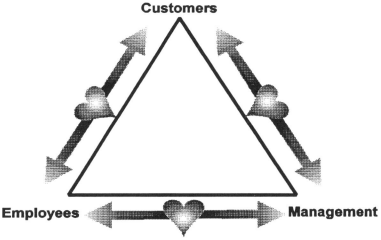

The Arteries of Effective Communication

For the business to be sustained, effective two-way communication must take place between each apex of the pyramid.

Management communicates the requirements of the job to employees, so they will know what is expected of them. In the well run company, the employees are able to give feedback to management which will be used to improve products and conditions. Customers also communicate with the employees; placing their orders, spelling out delivery requirements, etc. Management communicates back and forth with customers when they do surveys, provide customer service functions, etc.

These lines of communication are arteries. The blood that flows through corporate arteries gives life to the business. If communication becomes blocked we have a corporate heart attack. If managers and employees don't talk, we have unhappy and ineffective employees; an employee heart attack. If customers can't talk with someone, no sales are made, and the customers just drift away; a customer heart attack. And if management can't or won't talk to the customers, they will not have the right products. Blockage in communication arteries quickly leads to organizational death.

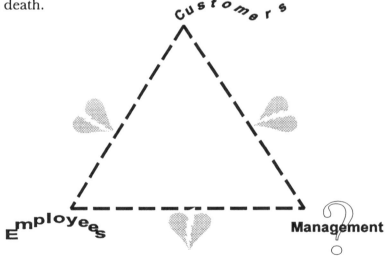

The Corporate Heart Attack
Results from Clogged Arteries

These heart attacks are killing more companies than all the competition could ever do with their advertising or lower prices. As Walt Kelly's Pogo says, "I have seen the enemy and he is us."

INTERNAL COMMUNICATIONS

Even when management knows what ought to be done to turn the company around and henceforth produce quality products or services, the effort is meaningless until this message is ingrained in the mind of every employee. In other words "decisions" of management must be turned into "clear requirements."

Do you remember, as a child, playing "telephone"? In business, it goes like this: a brief story (the directions) is whispered into the ear of the first person in the chain, and then the message is transferred along the links. Although not whispered, this is how many organizations communicate directions. Unfortunately, the end result, as is the case in the child's game, is usually skewed or totally out of reality with the original communication.

Often, after the mis-communication is finally discovered (and after a certain amount of revenue loss has already taken place), a subsequent communique is launched in the same manner and the ensuing garble is compounded and the revenue loss accelerated exponentially!

If this is the age of advanced communication technology—when we have television, telex, computer modems, satellites, and fax machines (and God forbid you're without your cellular phone)—why do some managers cling to outmoded ways of getting requirements to the people who need to understand them?

The most common and obvious method to alleviate confused directions is to write things down. Having said this, it's apparent immediately that written directions take time and effort. Without clarity, they often create even more problems. Ask your people:

- · Who writes directions?
- · Who receives directions?
- · Who keeps directions?
- · Who doesn't get the message?
- · Who doesn't read it?
- · Who understands what it says?
- · Who understands *differently* what it says?

Have you ever seen one of these signs?

CONFUSING LANGUAGE

The first and most important thing to understand in communicating information is that in any organization of more than one individual, multiple languages are spoken. It's not that we don't speak English (or American) or whatever language is generic to the organization's nationality. Imagine the problems multinational corporations face when many languages or dialects are spoken. That they can accomplish *any* semblance of quality communications is a miracle, given the fact it's so difficult to establish a meaningful transmission of data utilizing the *same* geographic language.

I remember some years ago when I learned to play Contract Bridge. Up to that point, I had never played card games, although I was vaguely aware of what a deck of cards looked like. But at my first lesson, the instructor began to talk about spades, hearts, diamonds, and clubs in ways that I couldn't associate with the ordinary meaning of these words. Then came bids, rebids, overbids, doubles, passes, dummies, finesses, revokes and vulnerability. I thought I'd come across a strange kind of foreign language.

That was the language of Bridge, and I have yet to work in a sector of business or government that doesn't have its own language or set of buzz words. Medicine, law, banking, fire-fighting, insurance, printing, real estate, restaurants, hotels... each has its own well-worn, mysterious, sometimes necessary, but always indigenous, language. If you're familiar with comput-ers—and who isn't these days?—remember the confusion that reigned when you first heard the computer-literate speak about floppy disks, macros, bits, bytes, RAM, ROM, software, booting and crashing?

Even the quality business is guilty. We have SQC (statistical quality control), SPC (statistical process control), SLA (service level agreement), JIT (just in time), TQC (total quality control), and enough others to write our own dictionary. I call them "bur-funkels."

Some years ago, a group of us invented "burfunkels" to describe those buzzwords that used to dismay and often frustrate us. From the beginning of my corporate experience, I've heard the "gobbledygook" come and go, sat in meetings with the "extrapolations," the "caveats," and more recently the "theory of constraints." I've come to the conclusion that use of these fifty-dollar words is not only unnecessary, but is foisted on us by a select group of corporate academicians who insist on developing a language that empowers them and makes others feel left out, less than, or just plain stupid.

When I was promoted from regional manager to vice president of A-M International, the president of the division informed me that I would report on a "tituary" basis for a short period of time. I rushed home to share this wonderful news with my wife, and together we spent a number of hours looking through dictionaries and encyclopedias and asking people what "tituary" meant.

The next morning I trotted into the president's office and asked him. And guess what? He didn't know what it meant, either; he just thought it sounded appropriate at the time. I learned later that he doted on odd and multi-syllable words, and was even known to have used "archaeopteryx" (a primitive bird with reptilian characteristics) in meeting conversations. The six vice presidents in the room at the time were impressed, but hadn't a clue what he was talking about and weren't about to ask.

The simple rule about communicating is to establish a global language which allows us to dictate policy and procedures within the organization and its vendors, customers and peers. When a common language is used—whether written or spoken—to communicate directions, all parties must understand the meaning of the information.

Jose Garcia, who teaches in business and government, as well as the field of education, has taught us that cultural diversity goes way beyond a simple language barrier. Maintaining a high level of communication with employees involves becoming conscious of, and sometimes addressing, others' cultural differences. Jose now gives cultural diversity training to Quality Concepts' clients.

An investment in this kind of procedure will reduce costs, improve morale and enhance sharing the mission with the members of the team. Sounds simple. Actually it is simple; it just isn't easy.

It's understandable, then, that some organizations haven't gotten the message, as it were, and the result is some verbal, some written, and mostly guessed communications and lots of

doin' it over again!

COUNT THE "F"s

One of the chief barriers to effective communication is the belief that we think we already know what's going to be communicated. To reveal this tendency, I often give a simple test at my workshops. I ask the students to count the "F's" in the sentence below. They're not allowed to read through it twice.

"Finished files are the result of years of scientific study combined with the experience of many years."

How many "F"s do *you* see? The lowest answer is usually "three" and more people give that number than any other. A few say "four" or "five," but there are actually six. Why did they fail to see all of them? Because three of them are in the word "of." This is such a little word, we sometimes don't see it. We have this multi-billion-dollar device in our heads, but we sometimes need a software update. We have the late Evelyn Wood speed-reading classes to go faster and faster, but most of the time we pay a price for speed.

We often forget the most important part of communicating is listening. You've heard the old saying, "Better to keep silent and be thought a fool, than open your mouth and remove all doubt."

In *Rude Awakening* (Morrow, 1989), a fascinating book about General Motors, author Mary Ann Keller talks about Ross Perot. His computer company was bought by GM and he got a seat on the board. One day they decided to set up a task force to study why their paint jobs didn't hold up as well as those on Japanese cars. Perot left the office on the 14th floor, went over to the paint shop and asked one of the guys on the line. And he said, "It's simple. Our cars are sprayed and their cars are dipped." You can solve a lot of problems by listening instead of talking. (But wise men don't talk to peasants!)

Incidentally, this simple incident was the beginning of the end for Ross Perot's relationship with GM; and they paid an additional $50 million to make Perot go away. Whose money was that?

There are still plenty of managers who think success is measured by the number of layers of glass between them and their people. They think isolation makes them important; the truth is it only makes them unaware. Like the Lone Ranger's faithful Indian companion, Tonto, a manager needs to put his ear to the ground if he wants to learn what's happening.

It's no secret that business organizations fail every day. To keep that from happening to them, in February, 1991, the Capital Bank in Miami began a quality process. They gathered over three hundred people together at the Omni Hotel and the chairman, CEO and other managers explained that, although change was afoot, they needn't be afraid. They explained to the employees three important phases:

1. Where were we?
2. Where are we?
3. Where are we going?

In 1992, seven hundred employees attended the second annual All-Hands Meeting; and in March of 1993, '94 and '95, the meetings were again jam-packed with over 800 excited, enthusiastic partners in their quality process. The results are pride as well as profits.

Another company I worked with makes a small part that goes into the reentry system of the space shuttle. The owner thought this was important and he wanted his employees to know the value of building quality into that small part. So he took them all out to the parking lot at Edwards Air Force Base. It was very early in the morning, still dark, and he gave them breakfast and coffee and had them wait for the shuttle to come in.

He made a short speech: "If we don't do our jobs right, the parts will be defective, the reentry system will fail and the shuttle won't come back. It will just go off in space."

Everyone was silent, staring into the sky, waiting for the sound of the shuttle. And then it came: a sonic boom as it entered the atmosphere. The employees applauded, yelled, jumped up and down and hugged one another. There were even tears in some eyes.

What do *you* do? Who uses the products you make: schools, lawyers, pilots, doctors, Olympic organizers? Whatever product or service you provide, no matter how small, it helps these people do their jobs. You may not make the space shuttle come back safely, but if what you make helps some people do their jobs better, you contribute.

Your employees need to know where they fit in. Leaders communicate that message to them in a graphic manner.

COMMUNICATING WITH CUSTOMERS

When I was working to become a successful sales representative, I used to read the books and listen to the records of a man named Clement Stone, who was the most successful insurance salesman in the world. He was making a point about not talking so much that we talk ourselves out of a sale, and he shouted, "Once you've made the presentation, then shut up!!! And listen to what the customer is gonna say. The next person to talk is the loser." One story he told was of the first presentation of a million dollar policy in the '30's; and after he made his pitch, he and the prospect sat for 20 minutes without a word. Finally, the prospect broke out laughing and signed the deal. Patience.

It's not surprising that where companies often go wrong is in communications with customers. We don't shut up and listen. If you don't know what the customer wants, you can't provide it, in perfect working order and on time. Unfortunately, the customer doesn't always speak your language. When a customer goes into a printing shop to have some letterhead made, she knows what she wants, but doesn't speak "printerese." This allows for plenty of mistakes between what she thinks she said and what you think she said. Sometimes we "assume," and you know what that does: it makes an ass out of you and me.

ASS-U-ME

Sometimes a customer changes an order. Maybe he's always asked for his letterhead to be printed in black ink on white paper. But this time he's making a change and he wants blue ink. If you "assume" this order is like the others, you're in for a big shock. The work is wrong and we get to

do it over again.

And you have an unhappy customer besides, one whose business may go elsewhere next time.

We can't afford to assume we know; we have to make sure. Suppose you went to a doctor and he didn't know what you really wanted, but cut you open anyway and removed something and it was the wrong thing? How would you feel? Would you feel any better if he said, "Can you accept it this one time?" or "I'll give you 10 percent off," or "Well, I'll re-operate."?

We need to understand the requirements of our customers in order to perform quality work. The surgeon, the engineer, the pressman or the bank teller—in fact, all businesses—serve customers; and it's imperative to understand their requirements in order to satisfy them, keep them coming back and have them tell others about the high quality of our work.

The requirements are what set the standard for the job. Without requirements, we are at best guessing what our customers want. When they don't know what their specific requirements are, we must use our communication skills to determine what it is they need and what will satisfy them.

One of my favorite stories has to do with the man who told a doctor he wanted to be castrated. The doctor tried to talk him out of it but he insisted he knew what he wanted. When he came out of the anaesthetic, he noticed another man about to enter the operating room. "What are you going in for?" he asked.

"Circumcision," the other man said.

"Oh, my God, *that* was the word!"

I sometimes think of a customer as an onion that needs to be peeled down. You remove one layer at a time until you reach the pearl of truth at the center, which is what the customer wants. To do this you ask questions, you communicate. You don't force your standards on customers. Have you ever heard someone say, "That's the way we do it and if you don't like it..."? The customer doesn't have to like it; the customer can go elsewhere.

One way to be sure you know what the customer wants is to ask for a sample. The FAX machine has been an incredibly helpful component in doing it right the first time. You've got to teach your employees to ask basic questions. You know the questions to ask; communicate with them. Do you ever conduct a survey of what your customers want? I call it the "How Are We Doing?" report. Don't wait until you suddenly realize that one of your oldest and best customers hasn't been around in six months. When the customer walks in the door, hand him this question-naire, with only three short questions on it and say, "Would you mind filling this out while we're preparing your order?" Most customers won't mind; in fact they're flattered that you want to know what they think. You'd be surprised to know how many customers *wish* a company would give them an opportunity to say what they think!

The three questions are:

> 1. How do we rate on a scale of 1 to 5?
> 2. Rate our best competitor on the same scale.
> 3. How could we serve you better?

It's when the customers don't know what they want that we become true professionals in our industry. Customers may not know what all their options are. Lately restaurants are training their waiters and waitresses to offer more than what the customer has ordered. "Would you like to start with one of our special appetizers?" "May I show you the dessert tray?" Even at fast-food outlets, the order-taker may say, "Would you like fries with that?" Once we explain the options, the customer can make a more informed decision, and we might make additional sales. As the trusted experts who guide and direct them toward a product that will satisfy their needs, we earn satisfaction, repeat business, an excellent reputation, opportunities for growth, and pride.

JOIN THE DOTS

Place the tip of a pencil on the dot at the upper left hand corner, and without lifting the pencil or reversing direction, go through all nine dots with four straight lines.

```
●   ●   ●

●   ●   ●

●   ●   ●
```

This is a test I give to workshop attendees. It's been around for years, but it illustrates the point that most people automatically assume they're constrained by the pattern, even though there was no warning to stay within it.

The trick, of course, is to go *outside* the dots. In business, sometimes we must go outside the dots—that is, try new, imaginative ideas—to get a job done.

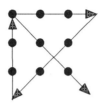

One day a customer drove in to a service and repair shop and discovered that the young man who normally ferried passengers to their offices while their cars were being serviced, was unable to get to work as scheduled, and all the loaner cars were already spoken for. The owner's implied promise to his customers was on the line and he had to solve the problem quickly, before the customer was late for work. He called the local taxi company and paid the fare, $17, in advance. He went outside the dots to satisfy a customer.

At the Do-It Center, if you return something, they'll give you your money back without question. When this concept was first suggested to them, managers were aghast. "We can't do that," they said, "we'll be ripped off." The old rules were that you distrusted the customer; you protected yourself from the possibility he might hurt you financially. After all, the aim was to make money, not lose it.

Don Shapiro, of First Concepts Development Corp. says, "Examine your own service policies. If they're based on the actions of the one percent of your customers who are dishonest instead of on the ninety-nine percent who are honest, then you have a problem."

But the system used by the home improvement store had another purpose. If you bring something back they give you your money, but they want to see your driver's license. This is *not* for the purpose of making a list of people who habitually bring things back and rip off the store. It's because the president then writes to the customer, asking why the product was returned. "What did we do wrong? How could we do it better? How was the over-all service?" At first the letters they got back were very negative; the customers complained about a lot of things at that store. But this told the managers where they had problems and they fixed them. Gradually the letters became complimentary. This happened because the managers *communicated* with the customers. Instead of going out of business for lack of satisfied customers, they fixed their problems and grew. The feedback literally went from "You stink!" to "You're great!" in eight months.

Sometimes you have to take risks. The syndicated advice columnist, Ann Landers, quoted this recently: "Don't be afraid to go out on a limb; that's where the good fruit is." Or, as Zero Mostel's character said in the film, *The Producers*, "He who hesitates is poor."

When Toyota designed the Lexus automobile, they sent engineers to southern California to live for awhile with American families who fit the niche market for their new product. They followed the Americans around, asking questions. When they learned what Californians wanted and needed in a car, they designed and built it, and earned a number one in the world rating by J. D. Powers & Associates, a recognized authority in automobile quality through customer satisfaction.

Look at Kentucky Fried Chicken and McDonald's. Long before these two companies became household words, people sold both chicken and hamburgers. What made them special? They did it differently; they went outside the dots. Colonel Sanders had a unique recipe for frying chicken, one that experience (communicating with the people who tasted it) told him would become popular.

Ray Kroc, who bought the McDonald brothers' hamburger stand in San Bernardino, California, knew that people wanted fast food. They not only wanted it fast, they wanted it good. He established Hamburger University in Illinois to teach his franchisees how to make the same good hamburgers and French fries every time. Kroc was a man of integrity as well as vision, and was one of the first to put women and minorities into management positions.

That's not all. If you put in an order at McDonald's and then change your mind, does the order-taker say, "I'm sorry; you can't do that; I already put your order in"? Or does he say, "Okay, I can do that"? The customer is always right. Even when he's wrong. Today you can buy McDonald hamburgers in Moscow and Paris. How's that for growth?

INTERVIEW with ZUMAR INDUSTRIES

In 1982, when Pete Lemcke and Norm Tardif took over Zumar Industries, which manufactures highway signs, the company had been in business since 1947 and quality of the product was not an issue. Production standards were high and there were few customer complaints.

However, as business expanded and Zumar grew from 17 employees to 35, other problems showed up. They were experiencing excessive absenteeism, tardiness, too much turnover, and poor communication between offices. To try to counteract this, the owners instituted a comprehensive health insurance program and profit sharing, together with a good vacation policy and generous holiday package; yet difficulties persisted.

As Norm Tardif tells it: "We weren't bad... but we wanted to be better.... Just at this time, Pete and I attended a breakfast meeting at a business conference we were enrolled in and the speaker was Bob Sherer of Quality Concepts. About 20 minutes into his program, a light went on. And it happened to both of us, because I looked at Pete and he looked at me and we just knew this was it. This was the tool. We didn't have a plan and Bob gave us the plan.

"Quality Concepts was hired to give quality communication workshops in both company locations, Tacoma and Los Angeles, plus an extra workshop in Los Angeles in Spanish."

They followed these up with surveys in both Spanish and English and the results were astounding. "I don't think any one part of this program has had more impact on our work force than doing that session in Spanish," Norm says.

In addition, their next newsletter contained an article in Spanish, not just for the Spanish-speaking employees, but so the English-only employees could see what it's like not to be able to read something they need to know about.

They next held special workshops for managers and have a management team which emphasizes quality in every phase of the business. The term "ZQ," which means Zumar Quality, has entered the company vocabulary, and people can be heard saying things like, "Well, I'll get together with a couple of the guys and we'll ZQ it."

Tardif says they didn't consider themselves a large enough company to have an Employee of the Month, but they do have a Star of the Quarter. "We have an extremely stringent criteria. One part is objective and the other is subjective; but if you don't ace the objective part, you're not considered. If you're Star of the Quarter, you really earned it. You get a cash reward, an engraved plaque, your own parking spot with a big gold star and your name and picture on it. People who came close, but didn't quite make it one quarter are called Rising Stars. At the end of the year, we consider all of these people as candidates for Super-Star of the Year. This award is given at our Christmas party, where the bosses supply, set up and prepare all the food, and even barbecue the steaks.

"Personal relationships have also improved with the quality process. For example, there had been Christmas parties before we started the program, but there was little inter-change among employees; each had his own little clique. But now we have blacks and whites and Asians and Hispanics all mixed up. Improved communications has made them feel like a team all working toward the same goal."

C.A.N.I. is a big thing at Zumar. It stands for Continuous And Never-ending Improvement, and employees are reminded of it frequently. Reducing it to a two-word phrase, Can I?, reinforces that idea. The vision statement, or philosophy of the company, below, has been put on several 36 x 45-inch aluminum signs and hung all over the building, again both in Spanish and English.

"There are lots of upstart companies that compete with us," Norm says, "and we know we can't stay ahead on price alone; so we empower our employees to make good decisions that will satisfy customers. But it's not enough to just institute a program; you have to go back often, constantly reinforce the message that this is important. But the results more than make up for the cost of the programs."

THE ZUMAR PHILOSOPHY

In order to be *Clearly the Best* in our business, we are committed to these principles:

The individual must be respected.

People, not money or things, are an organization's greatest asset. We want the people who work for us to feel good about themselves and their work. Each individual makes a difference. Superior performances are recognized and rewarded.

The customer must be given the best possible service.

In some way, every job relates to enhancing that goal. If you're not servicing the customer, then you should be servicing someone who is. Outstanding products and service are what keep bringing customers back to do more business.

Excellence and superior performance must be pursued.

Pursue all tasks with the idea that they can be accomplished in a superior fashion. To achieve excellence, we need superior training, and we must feel compelled to succeed. A highly competitive environment creates an atmosphere that nurtures excellence.

These principles must be accepted by each employee and be the basis for our behavior and performance. It is not how big we are that is important. It is how good we are.

Challenge: What will you do to improve communications in your organization?

_____

_____

_____

_____

_____

_____

_____

_____

_____

_____

_____

_____

_____

_____

_____

_____

_____

_____

10

DO YOU KNOW YOUR CUSTOMERS?

The customer who's always right probably waits on himself.

Laurence J. Peter

I n one of her usual witty syndicated columns, the well-known American humorist, Erma Bombeck, said: "I read a story the other day about trends, which said that in order to bring more business to the marketplace, salespeople are going to focus on being more polite and give good service. What will they think of next? Speaking as a consumer, it's been a while since merchants wanted our business badly enough to smile for it. Gone are the days when banks used to give us blenders for opening a new account and gas stations seduced us with matching glasses when we changed our oil. Some of us even remember furnishing our homes in early Green Stamps.

"Then," Bombeck says, "it all went away... you pumped your own gas, and a band of nomads called 'shoppers' wandered from counter to counter dragging their purchases and shouting, 'Is there anyone here who can help me?' Self-service entered our lives... Like most shoppers I yearn for the day when we can enter a fitting room with garments over our arm and not be treated as an escaped felon... without alarms going off, security trellises to walk through and a plastic clamp dangling between my knees like an anchor."

One of the first things I do when I go into a company is talk to employees about their customers. And some of them tell me,

"I don't deal with customers. I never deal with customers. I don't want to deal with them."

So let's get one thing straight at the beginning: we *all* have customers. The sales reps, the people in the front of the store, have *external* customers; but everyone in the organization *is* a customer and has *internal* customers. Some have both. This isn't new; you've heard it before. But it bears repeating. It also needs more emphasis than it's been receiving and a few suggestions (which you'll find later on) about how to satisfy that internal customer so that the product goes out perfectly, and on time, to that external customer.

CUSTOMER STUPIDITY

The customer is *always* right, even when he's wrong!

The most amazing thing about some employees is that, when offered the opportunity to express what would make their job more fulfilling, or help the company to perform better, their first and immediate suggestion is to get rid of problem customers, or to distance themselves from customer interaction. This is gloomy news indeed for a nation that has lost so much of its employment to offshore interests.

When polled, a recent group of employees went so far as to indicate that, if only customers would leave them alone, they could get their jobs done. Guess what? It's *guaranteed* the customers will, and probably are, leaving them alone in ever increasing numbers. And their jobs *will* soon be done. Forever.

"But some customers are more trouble than they're worth. They cause problems." Nonsense. There are no problem customers; there are only customers who haven't had their needs met correctly, on time, and with courtesy. Too often the customer who comes in with a chip on his shoulder the size of a redwood is one who has been treated so badly by others that he expects poor treatment and being defensive is his only weapon in the battle to get what he wants and deserves.

Throughout the many market niches we cover while working with clients, there is one common denominator. The people on the front line perceive customers to be lacking in enough sense to come in out of the rain, much less to do business at their particular counter or desk. A counter person in a copy store comments, "These people are so stupid; they walked in here and asked if they could get a copy." A bank teller treats customers with disdain because they don't understand terms relative to the banking industry.

But it's *your* job to educate customers about your business. We often ask managers and owners to walk in their own front door and see the store or department through the eyes of their customer. They would then realize that inadequate signs and intimidating features deter the customers and force them to ask obvious questions of the employees. In many cases, signs are of inadequate size, confusing, or set in the wrong places. Because employees understand what a sign means, they may have turned it sideways or backwards, and then ask the customer, "Didn't you see the sign?" or, in other words, "Are you stupid?"

The Do-It Center has done an extremely good job in this area. They have huge signs in their stores directing customers to specific areas, such as Hardware, Electrical, Paint, Garden, etc., and they have cleverly named each of their aisles. For instance, in the hardware section there is Screw Lane, Nail Street and Bolt Alley. These not only direct customers to what they need, but are fun for both them and employees, who get a kick out of erecting the signs and are more apt to remember where the materials are themselves.

If quality begins on the front line—the first customer contact—then an appropriate amount of money, at least as much as your advertising budget, should be spent teaching customers how to "be smart" in your facility. By instructing your employees, your graphics department or your facilities management how to do a better job of directing customers, you'll provide (to borrow a well-worn computer term) a "user friendly" atmosphere. Customers will return again and again to the company which provides this climate.

Customers ask questions such as, "Can I get a copy?" in a copy store, or "Can I get my teeth cleaned?" in a dentist's office because of many years of poor service from business and hearing things like, "No, you can't get a copy unless it's between one and three on Thursday and then only on pink paper," or, "No, doctor doesn't see people without references from six other patients." Are you doing everything possible in *your* company to eliminate customer stupidity, or are you fueling it through poor signage, no signage or inept employees who persist in thinking customers are a sub-form of human life?

Four out of five businesses fail in their first year, not because of lack of sufficient capital, or a bad business plan. They fail because they had an insufficient number of customers. Customers are the life blood of any organization; moreover customer service and satisfaction is the only defensible justification for any organization's existence. This is why getting and keeping customers today has become a real dilemma for those companies whose employees regard the customer as a nuisance.

Any organization funded by customer transactions, or contributions, or even taxes, has customers. This includes the local department store, bank and insurance company, the welfare assistance office and the department of motor vehicles. Businesses are rarely founded just to create jobs, as some employees believe; rather they are chartered to attract and serve customers, with the end objective being profits. Jobs do not create customers. The reverse is true. Providing responsive service to the customer is the only reason any job exists. Unfortunately, many employees, managers and staff members tend to look on the customer as an intrusion into their perceived priority of work requirements.

Examples of this attitude abound: frustrated purchasers and seekers of service are left to fend for themselves. They're made to wait in interminable lines. They're ignored—and even avoided—by employees engulfed in functions other than attending to the needs of the customers.

Have you, or one of your employees ever said to a customer, "I'm sorry, we're closed. Come back tomorrow."? Would it surprise you to know that in many retail outlets, even today, the clerks couldn't care less if a customer dropped dead in the aisle? One of my workshop attendees added, "I know a store where this could take place and the dead person wouldn't be found for three days!"

Clerks who engage in private chats with other employees—while the customer builds up steam—only serve to confirm this lack of concern for customers. From the customer's point of view, not only is the employee at fault, but more importantly, the management, and the organization as a whole, are perceived as being responsible for inadequate service. And they're right. It's not just a clerk or server issue. It's incumbent upon management to hire, train, and promote employees who will offer a level of excellence that customers will seek out and return for again and again.

MORE HOURS, LESS SERVICE

It's difficult to fathom the logic of an organization's decision to expand its hours of operation, only to offer poor service, or *no* service. It's like spreading disease: "Gee, we're doing all these wrong things in only eight hours; let's see how much we can do in twelve hours."

The possibility of repeat business hinges on each customer's level of satisfaction with service. When the customer is ignored and neglected, and served only after tracking down a reluctant employee who professes to know nothing, or shirks responsibility with, "It's not my job, but I'll do you a favor..." the likelihood of repeat business fades into oblivion.

Customer recruitment is one of the simplest and most fundamental elements of business. The basics haven't changed since the beginning of commerce.

- Offer a product or service.
- Assure value for the customer's investment.
- Treat the customer with dignity and respect.

These things are not hard to do; yet every surreptitious plan imaginable has been invented by employees and management to circumvent offering these simple sought-after business basics. For example, how often have you been enticed into a place of business with catchy slogans, sophisticated advertisements, or offers of incredible bargains, led to believe you're about to acquire the deal of the century? But when you enter the store, there's no one to wait on you, and when you finally find someone, he responds, "What ad?"

This departure from business basics is amazing when we see evidence of some organizations who do little or no physical advertising, yet enjoy a land-office business. Their customers guarantee the best possible form of advertising, the satisfied customer, third party endorsement. One well-known department store receives millions of dollars in *free* advertising every day simply by following the basic business rules. Yes, the department store is Nordstrom. When you open a newspaper, you see advertisements from every other major department store chain, but not Nordstrom. Instead, they put that money into training their employees to provide excellent service.

When employees regard customers as a nuisance or intrusion, you can be sure this attitude flows directly from management. Only managers can change the perspective of the work force, and then only by changing their own attitude first.

The most significant business arena left for employment in America is in the service sector. That's right: serving customers. Over 75 percent of jobs in this country today are service-oriented. If this trend continues, it's estimated that by the year 2000 over 90 percent of the jobs in America will be service-oriented. Think about it. Banks, insurance companies and tax-supported service organizations must aggressively attack the issue of training employees to understand that, without good service, there will be no customers and without customers, there will be no need for that business and its employees.

Having enjoyed a good run at American markets in automobiles, sewing machines, electronics and computers, the Japanese are now turning to our service industry. When they buy up our farms, our office buildings and our food franchises, some people say, "Not to worry; they can't take them out of the country!" But they do take the *profits* out of the country.

Unfortunately, sometimes, after finding someone to wait on them in a store, the customers' problems have only begun. Some sales people are so poorly trained they have no idea of the stock they're responsible for.

A friend of mine was in a book store not long ago and asked for a particular title by name and author. The clerk turned immediately to the computer and, after what seemed like forever, returned to inform her that they didn't have that book; in fact, no such book was listed under Books in Print. After several abortive attempts to locate the book under some other category, the owner of the shop finally appeared and asked if he could help. My friend repeated her request and his clerk told him of his fruitless search. The owner went to the shelves where books of that kind might be found, picked one up, and said, "This is similar; would it be of any help to you?" It turned out to be the exact book she was looking for! The problem was not with the original request or with the computer, but with the clerk, who, when told the author's name was Syd Field, was looking under "S."

The Book Store, an independent store in San Mateo, California, is an example of how things *should* work. In this store everyone was so familiar with the stock that customers had only to give the vaguest hint of the book they were looking for. The clerks would invariably come up with the correct title, go immediately to the shelves and pull it out! It's no wonder they were in business for over 30 years in spite of all the competition from the big chain bookstores.

Another example is the owner of a flower company who says that she has "only two products: flowers and service." Since flowers are so often gifts, and her employees must write messages for the enclosed greeting cards, she makes sure they know how to spell and their handwriting is legible.

COURTESY

If you would have a successful business, repeat this aloud a hundred times a day: The customers are always right, even when they're wrong. If I put my hand up and ask you to put yours up against it, and then apply the slightest amount of pressure, what will happen? You can do this with anyone and the result is the same; the other person begins to push back. When the customer says, "You didn't do this right," and you say, "I did," you're like the hand pushing back. Then the customer says, "You didn't," and you say, "I did," and pretty soon you have your own version of World War III, and a corporate heart attack.

All customers like to be treated with courtesy, and one of the easiest things to do is teach your employees to smile. When someone smiles at you, it's second nature to smile back. Even on the telephone, "service with a smile" still counts for a lot.

Some managers have made efforts to make their customers feel like "one of the family," for example by calling customers by name. It's easy to do because their name is visible on their check or credit card. It just takes training and caring. It's always flattering to be remembered. When you go into a bank for the third time and the teller now recognizes you and calls you by name, you feel they really care about your business.

On the other hand, excessive familiarity is a turn-off.

A dentist lost a potential new client when his receptionist, a girl barely out of her teens, insisted on addressing the new patient, a man of clearly mature age, by his first name. A department store received an irate letter from a woman customer who, while obviously old enough to be the clerk's mother and previously unknown to her, was called by her first name three times within the two-minute sales transaction. It is never rude to use a person's last name; use his or her first name—unless asked to do so—at your peril.

But many people, thus offended, won't write letters, won't tell you what irritated them; they simply take their business to another store.

TELEPHONE BLUES

Not every business deals face-to-face with customers. Some retail businesses are conducted through mail or telephone orders and many other services depend largely on the telephone. Yet the managers of those companies have no idea of the trauma they inflict on their customers and clients by poor use of this means of communication.

In some companies, Voice Mail has replaced an operator, and you will not speak to a human being for a considerable length of time. You get a recorded message to hit certain buttons on your touch-tone phone depending on the department you want. If you're not sure, you're required to listen to the entire message, and information about nine other departments, before you find the one you want. If ever. Irate customers have complained they've been in Voice Mail Jail, gone around and around and never got out of a vicious circle of recorded messages. Gordon

Matthews, who invented voice mail and first marketed the system in 1980, says this was not what he had in mind. Matthews' idea was to replace internal company memos and solve the problem of "telephone tag" and busy signals. The current problems with it stem from the way various companies use it.

The system, as currently practiced, saves the company money because they now use fewer employees. But, unless you're the I.R.S., and the customer has no choice but to deal with you, such practices may leave you with fewer customers as well as fewer employees. It's understandable that companies need to control costs, and employees cost money; but whenever a company chooses to reduce telephone operators—or other staff—their obligation to train the remaining employees for courtesy and true service becomes that much greater.

Communications Briefing, a Blackwood, N.J. newsletter, recently listed important points for voice mail etiquette:

- Greetings should be short, friendly and slow enough to understand.
- Menu options should be in order of popularity so most people don't have to listen to a long list first.
- Make talking to a live operator one of the first options on the menu.
- Try the system yourself to find out if what you thought was efficient may be annoying to your customers.

In a growing number of telephone transactions, customers are required to wait on hold while music is played at them. The music is either piped in or someone hooks up a radio to the system. It's bad enough to be a captive audience and have to listen to someone else's idea of music; but totally intolerable when they've connected a radio and you must listen to station announcements and commercials! The owners and managers of these businesses seldom call their own numbers and probably have no idea what a customer must listen to, and why some of them might hang up and never call back!

Some companies have a simple, upbeat message indicating their additional product or service offerings, with a warm reassurance that you haven't been forgotten.

If I must be put on hold, I prefer silence during which time I can think, or do some other work on my desk. I am not paranoid enough—as some people seem to think when I've complained about the practice—to believe I've been cut off just because I have a few moments of silence. And if I have to wait *more* than a few moments, your company has another problem!

KEEPING CUSTOMERS

If you operate a retail business, are you aware of the music being played in your store? Many of today's clerks were raised in the era of loud rock and roll and, left alone in your store, will play it for their own amusement. If your store caters primarily to teenagers or young adults, that may be acceptable; however, the "Stones" may be the reason someone walks out of shoe stores, appliance stores, and especially restaurants, because the music was not only a turnoff but so loud that it made conversation difficult.

Even if your customers don't hear the music—such as in the back office or working area of your plant—you should be aware of the distraction it might cause. One of our clients banned radios from these areas because the competition for station selection, and the increased decibel levels, had taken the place of anything resembling work, much less quality work. He reports to us that his "no radios" policy brought productivity up and errors down!

The best of companies can have occasional customer problems. How they're handled often makes the difference between companies that remain in business and those that don't. Teaching your employees how to handle problems and resolve conflict is the most effective training you give. First, it's often wise to let the irate customer (internal or external) say all he wants to right up front, to blow off steam. Like the hand pushing back, it's second nature to want to interrupt the flow of complaints and give excuses, but that only adds fuel to the fire. When allowed to speak out, customers often cool off all by themselves. Empathy, blameless apology and listening will usually defuse the situation.

Next, it's vitally important to solve the problem as quickly as possible; delaying action only compounds it.

The four steps in problem solving are:

1.   Identify the problem. Find out exactly what caused the customer to complain.
2.   Evaluate it. Determine how serious it really is to both the customer and the company.
3.   Negotiate a satisfactory solution. Determine what will make the customer happy and try to fit company response to it.
4.   Take steps to complete it. Once a solution is found, be sure it's implemented as quickly as possible.

We all like to be treated with courtesy and we're all customers. A recent survey pointed out that if a customer is happy about your service, he'll tell eight people during the next twelve months, on average. But if he's unhappy, he'll tell 24 people. It sounds unfair, but it's fact. So when you make a customer unhappy, you'll soon have 24 other people who know about it. It takes a long time to attract and keep 24 new customers. In fact, it costs five times more to get one new customer than to keep a current one. That shows up on the bottom line.

Recently I was in Los Angeles speaking to a bank president. As we sat in his office on the 23rd floor, we could look out of his window and see people going in and out of the door. The president said to me, "We don't have trouble getting them in the front door. Our concern is what happens once they're inside."

What happens to customers after they come in the front door determines whether they'll return and establish a long-term relationship. As leaders of business today, we have to ask ourselves: How much money are we spending to get new customers? How much are we willing to spend to keep the current customers? Unfortunately, once we've got them, we tend to take them for granted, like spouses, children and friends. Our employees need to know that our current customers are valuable, and they must work hard to keep them.

SERVICE

Customers have repeatedly shown that they will pay more for good service. Another example came to light in Paul B. Brown's article about Direct Tire and Sales, a Boston company, in *Inc*. Magazine.

In it, Brown reports that Direct Tire Sales president, Barry Steinberg, admits his prices are 10 or 12 percent higher than "just about everybody." So what keeps the customers coming back? It's because he offers superior service.

"Need to buy some tires and be in and out in an hour? No problem... Can't wait? No big deal. Take one of the company's seven loaners to work, and pick up your car on the way home. And what if those new tires blow out after 30,000 miles or you decide after a month that you flat out don't like them? No sweat. Steinberg guarantees the tires, as well as any service work his shop does - forever."

Customers want companies to perform as they say they will, to keep their promises. If that means stocking more inventory than anyone else, that's what you do. If it means providing a service to store snow tires in the summer, you do that too. Besides loaner cars, Steinberg also provides fresh magazines and fresh coffee in his waiting room; and since he wants to project a professional image, he provides his employees with the uniforms they wear.

University National Bank & Trust Co., in Palo Alto, California, is an institution that provides exceptional service to its customers. Writing in *Nation's Business*, author Joan C. Szabo reported that the bank "performs services such as sending messengers to pick up deposits, arranging after-hours appointments for business managers too busy to get to the bank during regular hours,... and notifying customers of overdrafts instead of bouncing their checks and imposing penalties."

What a contrast between that bank and the one a friend of mine recently parted company with. Because my friend got paid on Friday nights, he liked being able to go to the bank between five and six p.m. on Fridays. Suddenly his bank changed its hours to 9 a.m. to 5 p.m., with no more late openings. He talked to the bank personnel who told him it was temporary, an experiment. So he waited to see if the policy would change back. For six months he had to change his habits and not do his banking until his lunch hour the following Monday. But at the end of six months, the policy was still in effect. He changed banks, going to one that stayed open until 6 p.m. on Fridays. Ironically, a year later, the first bank not only began staying open Friday nights again, they announced Saturday morning openings as well, all in an attempt to regain the customers they lost by their former ill-considered change. A customer survey in advance might have saved them a lot of grief, to say nothing of revenue.

The company my friend moved his accounts to was one which had had a fire in their Los Angeles offices. In spite of the devastation of that fire, not a single record, not a day's business, was lost. He felt that any company that was so well prepared for such a catastrophe must be well managed and would be a safe place for his money.

One definition of good service is doing things for customers the way they would do them if given the opportunity, to seek the customer point of view. As one successful company president says, "Don't try to judge or label your customers as 'difficult' or 'impossible.' Look for ways to solve problems and find new and better ways to satisfy their needs." When you do that, the problem customer turns into a satisfied one. And everybody wins!

INTERNAL CUSTOMERS

Unless you're a one-person business, there are both external and internal customers. Employees who don't deal directly with the external kind are often ignorant of the fact that their fellow employees are their customers. The loader on the shipping dock is the customer of the person who hands him the carton to be shipped. (He can't ship the right article if he's given the wrong one.) The carton packer is the customer of the individual who provided him with the parts to be packed. The assembler is the customer of the various people who handed him the parts to be assembled. The order entry person is the customer of the salesman who took the order and passed on the information. The head of the department is the customer of the assistant who makes her appointments.

The external customer will not be served properly if employees don't treat their internal customers with respect and courtesy. If they don't have enough pride in their work to give their internal customers the right product or service at the right time, an inferior or defective—or somebody else's!—product gets shipped out the door to the external customer. And then, guess what? We get to

do it over again!

The larger the company, the more opportunity for internal customer problems. Creating separate divisions or departments can sometimes lead to finger pointing and blame placing instead of teamwork and craftsmanship. This is not to say that specialization is wrong; obviously the accounting department should be responsible for the fiscal side of the house, and sales people need to focus on producing orders. These separate areas are necessary and ensure that experts will address specific areas of responsibility.

But these "little companies" inside the larger one sometimes cause more trouble, leading to higher cost and loss of service to customers, than their competitors could ever hope to achieve!

Ask the order processors who handle the salesman's version of a completed order. Listen to secretaries who don't speak to each other due to departmental snobbery. Observe the head bashing between Marketing and Manufacturing. All of this havoc leads to the "not my job" mentality at the very least, and to the destructive lack of cooperation that leads to

doing it over again.

Even worse, when departments consider themselves fiefdoms, and perceive their importance to the company justifies ever larger staffs and ever bigger annual budgets, productivity, and ultimately, profit, flies out the window.

The blame for this state of affairs rests with high-level managers who set goals that pit one group against another to create internal competition. This philosophy was widely used in the '50's and '60's under the assumption that such competition would cause productivity to rise and be reflected on the bottom line. What actually happened is that warfare developed, with each department out to steal manpower, floor space and financial resources for themselves at great cost and disturbance to the total achievement of the company.

Further, some senior managers couldn't stand the thought of team building for fear that a strong team would plot to overthrow the throne. They created an atmosphere in which staff members were constantly vying with each other for the attention of the senior manager and doing anything to make themselves look good. They feigned support and togetherness, only to turn around and plunge a knife into the back of a fellow manager. Meanwhile, who's looking out for the customer? Remember the graphic of the ACME Company back in chapter five—how they *really* work? Sound familiar?

For the rank and file of workers, this show is better than *60 Minutes* or *Friends*. Their days are full of, "Did you hear what so-and-so did?" Chief executives, on the other hand, never seem to know what's so freely shared on line, through E-mail, the telephone or the FAX machine. Daniel Holtz, President of Capital Bank, told me the jungle drums reach everywhere in the organization except his office. It takes a dedicated chief executive to ferret out this kind of negative behavior and stop it before company morale, and possibly customer relations, are affected.

The managers who spend their time feathering their own nests, sucking up to the executive secretary or the administrative assistant to get the inside track with the CEO and wreak havoc among their fellow managers can only be spotted by sharp executives who can see through these tactics. They must institute a program in which harming another individual or division in the company will defeat that manager's goals. "All for one and one for all," did not end with the Three Musketeers; it's the only way to assure quality communications and internal customer service that guarantees external customers' loyalty.

A company is only as strong as its weakest link, and a strong CEO will establish methods that strengthen every link. One simple and effective tool is to assure each division within the company that it can't win without assisting in activities that help other departments. For example, the marketing department can't win without developing sales tools that help the sales department. The sales department can't get raises unless they turn in sales orders which are timely, easily understood and call for products within the scope of the company to provide. The order entry department can't earn bonuses without feeding the same high quality information to manufacturing, distribution and so on.

Engineering and manufacturing can't win when they fail to produce what the salespeople had been led to expect.

Successful leaders see to it that employees are not just doing their jobs, but are getting along well with their internal customers. They're all human; they have personal problems, ideals, plans for the future. Yet, cooperation is necessary. They need to be reminded that the competition is not *inside* the company, but outside. They don't need to draw chalk lines on the floor or build walls to keep others out. They're not in a life-or-death struggle to do something at the expense of another employee. Rather they're all in the same boat, and they need to row in the same direction or none of them will reach shore.

Remember that 30 to 35 percent of a company's operational costs are spent on having to redo work, a tremendous waste of capital and manpower. The progressive manager sees that teams work together to produce a product or service that satisfies the external customer and keeps everyone on the job. That's what success is all about:

Doing the Right Thing.

Challenge: What will you do to improve customer service and make sure they're not ignored, annoyed or insulted?

_____

_____

_____

_____

_____

11

ERROR PREVENTION,
NOT DETECTION

The cautious seldom err.
Confucius

W e didn't really need the example of the Persian Gulf war or aid to Somalia to demonstrate the U.S. ability to solve problems with an all-out "blitz." We've always been that way. As a nation of individualists, we don't like to sit down and make plans unless we're backed into a corner and the deadline is tomorrow morning at six o'clock.

The PBS television series, "The Civil War," was instructive for showing how we can bumble along for months or years and still come out ahead. For almost three of the four years of the Civil War, the North lost almost every battle. The generals were totally inept, ignored reports of southern weaknesses, refused to act in a timely manner, failed to capitalize on their advantages, and retreated from battles they could easily have won. The South, on the other hand, although continually outnumbered, felt their cause was just. They had the will to win and allowed their generals to use daring and unconventional strategies. Eventually, of course, the North did defeat the South. They had superior numbers, factories that could turn out war materials, and better communication systems. In all our wars, when faced with the necessity, our people rally to the cause, provide the necessary tools and make the final push to victory. But at what cost? How many lives were lost needlessly before the tide turned?

In many businesses today, managers, like old Northern generals, wait until a crisis is reached before doing anything about it. Then they rush through the plant, screaming at the employees about how vital the job is, cause mass hysteria, risk heart attacks and eventually ship the blivet amidst groans and exhaustion. Then things settle down until the next crisis. But during those hectic, "I-need-it-now!" moments, how many errors went undetected and will result, a few days later, in the need to

do it over again?

ERROR PREVENTION

Error detection is when you hire someone to stand at the end of the assembly line and check the product. They call it quality control. But when you find errors there, the blivet is already broken. You call it waste. I call it expensive. It's the 30-35 percent of your money and next year's performance evaluation raise. It doesn't take a lot of talent to find out something is broken after it's broken. What takes talent and effort is keeping it from breaking in the first place, or, if it does, keeping it from escalating into a major catastrophe.

Error prevention is when everyone pays attention all along the route from order to invoice. If you're someone in the middle of the process, and you think it's wrong, don't just send it on to the next person. Stop! Tell someone you think it's wrong. Clean up the mess before ten more people work on it and spend still more money. Before it comes out at the end broken and you must

do it over again.

Why don't we get up, raise our hand and holler when something goes wrong? Fear. A woman told me recently that she raised her hand and was told to sit down and shut up. She'll never stop another problem that comes to her attention. Furthermore, no one she works with, who saw and heard what happened to her, will do it either.

Error prevention is about finding errors and fixing them as soon as possible. It's not about shutting up the whistle blowers. And it's definitely not about taking the people out and shooting them. There are no galley slaves anymore and you can't get production figures up if you bring in a guy with a whip! People are human and humans make mistakes. The problem is kept small if the person who makes the mistake is allowed to admit it and get on with doing the next one right. If you encourage employees to inspect critically for errors all along the line, to ask questions if they're not sure, and to understand that the money saved helps to insure the growth of the company and their job security, the chances that things will be done right the first time mount considerably.

PLANNING WORK AND WORKING THE PLAN

To some managers, making a plan means merely adopting the latest quality buzz word: vision. Or a mission statement. When pressed to express this, they spout slogans, like, "Quality First," or "We will sell no wine before its time." There must be more than saying the object of the company is to make money, which is at best obvious. But not enough to fire people's imagination and excitement.

You need to write down your goals. If you're going to Kansas City and you don't have a road map, you may end up in Chicago. It doesn't make any difference if you're going to Kansas City or trying to improve quality in your company. If you don't have a map, you can easily get lost. Your plan is your map. Write it down. It can be one line: "Where am I trying to go? Am I going to hire another person this year? Am I going to double my business? This is what I'm gonna do this week. This month. This quarter. This lifetime."

Then you've got to share your goals with other managers and other employees. Then they need to "buy in," preferably by having some input to your goal or plan. Some companies make a beautiful statement. They tack it up on a wall, emblazon it in gold, backlight it and blare it from the public address system. The trouble is nobody does what it says. Write it down in simple terms so that everyone can understand it. "Model the mission." That means don't just talk about what you plan to do; work toward it every day. If you don't live it yourself and explain it to the troops—if they don't know what this translates to in terms of their jobs, income and satisfaction—it's wasted effort.

The plan must be written down, be specific, and be reinforced periodically. Then it must be worked continually. Start off each morning by reading your plan and then see what you can do to move it forward. Each employee should use a daily "To-Do" list, like the one on the next page. That's the plan.

DO IT RIGHT THE FIRST TIME

The best quality statement any company can have is: We Do It Right the First Time. By adopting this, working at it, and constantly reinforcing it, you can turn employees into a cooperative team, do quality work, increase your customer base, and accelerate profits! Remember, it's simple. It just isn't easy.

Our society has become so accustomed to doing things over again that budgets and cost proposals actually build in factors to cover the assured event that errors will occur. Workers report that re-entering, reshipping, reordering, and cost overruns are not only accepted, but expected as an every day fact of life. When the leader isn't clear about what's to be achieved, the employee may be compelled to think, "I'll just keep doing it over until you decide what you want." Word processors encourage this kind of operation; it's okay to key in data which will change many times regardless of the expense involved. While there is a positive benefit to being able to "massage" or change data, the

Things to Do
Right The First Time
TODAY

_____, 19___

Today's Goal: _____

    Appointments/Meetings_____

    _____

    _____

    _____

Priority
A-B-C

Completed
Right

1. ___ _____ ☐

2. ___ _____ ☐

3. ___ _____ ☐

4. ___ _____ ☐

5. ___ _____ ☐

6. ___ _____ ☐

7. ___ _____ ☐

8. ___ _____ ☐

9. ___ _____ ☐

10.___ _____ ☐

NOTES, DATA, SUCCESSES, etc. _____

_____

_____

_____

process—if carried to extremes—severely reduces the opportunity for the workers to perform their task *once* and have the enjoyment of having done it right the first time.

We've generated a work ethic that says if it doesn't work by the third time, read the directions! This may be seen as humorous; but, often, in humor lies the real truth and the truth can sometimes be tragic. Unfortunately, many approach their personal tasks with the attitude that they'll earn Brownie points if they can figure it out on their own. Meanwhile the directions are in the trash can, and are sought only after much time and effort is wasted, and the product perhaps permanently damaged.

Without a clear road map, a plan stated up front and often, many employees are unsure of what the company does, where it started, why it's successful and what they were hired to do. Perhaps they didn't receive the directions, they didn't understand them, or they changed without notice.

In one of my recent surveys of people entering the work force, I found that the majority were motivated by two desires:

1. To move out of their parents' home and into a place of their own.
2. To purchase a vehicle, preferably a Porsche, Lexus or expensive truck.

With these materialistic short term goals as motivating factors for a large percentage of new workers, it's vitally important to teach them the directions, standards, or requirements of the function they're paid to perform, and what part they play in the overall success (or failure) of the company. This is the only hope to build *esprit de corps* within the organization and prevent needless errors.

Some employees are confused because they don't understand the directions and because they honestly want to do quality work and are under the impression that they'll either appear stupid by asking questions or chastised for taking too much time. Often this ends up with the "Christmas present" type of performance: "I thought this was what you'd like," or "I did it the way I hoped would make you happy." Obviously, if it's not right, the manager is not only not happy, but now the work needs to be

done over again.

Everyone needs the opportunity to earn what I call "psychic income," the feeling of gratification when you know your work is well done. This leads to the employee seeking more gratification from doing it right the first time and opens the path to creative innovation and building long-term competent quality employees and teamwork.

To some managers, making plans means bringing in efficiency experts with their clipboards and stop watches, measuring the time it takes to do a job and then insisting all workers adhere to these standards. To other managers, it means hiring a quality control officer who looks at the product as it comes off the assembly line and determines if it's right or not. In other words, practicing Error Detection.

True quality depends on Error Prevention. When employees are motivated to Do it Right the First Time, refuse to pass on shoddy or incorrect work to their internal customer, there's no need to have Inspector Number 56 standing at the end of the line.

The steps to the goal are:

- Infuse quality terminology into the language of your organization. For example: Prevention; Do it Right the First Time; Think.
- Reinforce the quality commitment at regular intervals.
- Stay close to the employees and reward those who are succeeding.
- Don't give up!

When the average American company spends 30 to 35 percent of its time doing things over again, a lot of waste goes into the trash can or the dumpster. I was talking to a group of bankers recently and the president of a bank in Beverly Hills stopped me and said, "Bob, I disagree with your numbers." My mind was racing, trying to remember the source of my figures, and he said, "At our bank, it's more like 50 percent of the time is spent doing things over."

Even if your company is excellent and experiences only a 10 to 15 percent error rate, imagine what would happen to the bottom line if you could eliminate even half of those errors. There would be no equipment expense, no additional work force to hire, no added commissions or advertising, just *profit*. Quality is the most profitable product in America today, whether you provide service or products. When you practice total quality:

You win!

Your employees win!

Your customers win!

America wins!

TURNING THE DIAL

So, by Monday morning we're all going to be perfect, right? Wrong!

We're all into fast food, one-hour eyeglasses, instant coffee, one-day cosmetic surgery. We want everything right now. Well, perfection doesn't happen overnight. Sure, you'll *begin* to improve tomorrow if you start thinking in terms of doing it right the first time; but I think of improving quality as being like an old-fashioned television dial. Remember when you had to turn the knob to change channels? Click, next channel. Click again, next channel.

Improving quality is like turning the dial one click at a time. If you spin the dial too fast, it can break; so can company cultures when changed too often or too quickly. Changing behavior takes time and planning. The slogan at Dana Corp., which makes automobile parts, is, "Continuous improvement requires continuous education." When Ford Motor Company started their progress campaign known as "Quality is Job One," it took them seven years to reach the point where they passed GM, and the employees continue to earn larger bonuses than GM employees. Some of Ford's vehicles are now rated among the best automobiles manufactured, in terms of customer satisfaction and defects per unit.

Excellence is at the top of the dial, and you move toward it one click at a time. But when you get there, you find out Excellence has moved on, and you have to keep going. Things change; what was excellent yesterday is no longer excellent today. It's notched up. The world changes, customer requirements change, companies change.

Performance can always be improved, and the ultimate responsibility for continually upgrading performance standards rests with the top executive, the CEO, president or general manager. The job can't be delegated. If the senior manager doesn't set the standards, then every other manager will set different ones. Furthermore, the message perceived will be that senior management doesn't really think it's all that important.

Elevating quality goals means studying the company's current position compared to where you want to be, determining methods to attain those goals and then making a plan. Sit down with managers and discuss these points with them. "What are your problems and what are you going to do about them?" "What did you do *this year* to make improvements?" Sometimes such discussions can lead to lively dialogue. Train managers not to become defensive or withdrawn. Persist in finding out how they feel about their role in quality improvement and convince them that honesty is the only way to really identify problem areas so they can be corrected. It's not the message, it's how you deliver it.

If you get your message across, you can tell someone to go to hell and he'll look forward to the trip!

Such scrutiny will inevitably identify managers who need help, but top performers always enjoy a challenge. They want to do better in an environment that expects and rewards good work. A company that tolerates the mediocre or poor performer destroys morale and employees will either adjust their own work to that lower level or find a company that will appreciate them.

Regardless of the size of your organization, you may need to shift these top performers to other sections or divisions. A good worker usually knows his job thoroughly within a year; after that, he may be merely repeating what he did before, become bored or get too comfortable in his rut. A rut, you know, is a grave with both ends kicked out. On the other hand, such changes must not be made without a great deal of investigation. Many managerial jobs can be switched with impunity; in other areas, change—for the sake of change—can be dangerous.

It's common practice in some companies to promote the most skilled person in a department to its head. If a superior engineer gets promoted to head of engineering, you may lose a good engineer and gain a poor manager. Furthermore, it's possible you made him unhappy because he loved engineering and hates managing. Laurence Peter phrased it best in *The Peter Principle*: "In a hierarchy, every employee tends to rise to his level of incompetence."

And what does incompetence lead to?

Doing it over!

K.I.S.S.

Everyone knows K.I.S.S. means "Keep It Simple, Sweetheart," (It used to be Stupid, but we're a kinder, gentler nation now) and companies looking to improve quality would do well to heed the advice. Too many layers of organization tend to clog up the arteries of communication and slow down productivity. Fewer layers of management—if they're properly trained—can lead to managers and employees taking more responsibility, making better decisions and being more accountable for results.

One company president found a simple way to get rid of excess layers of management bureaucracy: he just went down the list and eliminated every job that began with the word "assistant."

Too many layers of management can sometimes lead to lack of accountability; there's always another level to blame mistakes on. Like too many bystanders when someone is being mugged on the street, individuals fear to depart from the crowd and do something unusual. But a single person, coming upon a crime, is far more likely to come to the aid of the victim. In business, a single manager is likely to feel empowered and more accountable.

Large companies are particularly prone to "territorial rights" attitudes. The managers defend their little fiefdom, failing to realize that they're all climbing the mountain together, hooked, like mountain climbers, to the same ropes, and if one falls, they're all in jeopardy. Successful leaders see that divisions work in harmony instead of competition with one another. They may call in managers from one department to give advice and help to another department.

Another way management can keep quality improvements coming is to reward those who really work at it. Talk about keeping things simple! Paying employees what they're worth is the most basic rule of business. Nothing demoralizes more than getting praise for your work with no monetary reward at raise time. While employees shouldn't expect to be given extra compensation for just doing what they're supposed to do, wages should not be capped so that a superior employee is kept at the same salary level as everyone else in the department.

This is particularly true of receptionists, who are really critical pulse points in companies. Too often they are thought of only as a face and a pleasant voice and some companies aren't willing to pay much for those qualities. This leads to that person becoming unhappy and moving on, looking for advancement and increased salary. But the customers judge a company by that first contact. Managers should consider how much it really costs to replace the person who has become knowledgeable about the company and built up good will among customers. Do something—bonuses, stock options, go outside the nine dots—to keep a good employee.

ACCOUNTABILITY

A popular expression among parents after World War II was, "I want my kid to have everything I never had." Unfortunately, both individuals and society suffer when people are simply *given* things. Unless you *earn* something—dollars, titles, toys—you're not likely to appreciate it, understand its value and reap the joy of psychic income, that sense of possession that transcends the monetary and brings a deep satisfaction.

Quality of work, and, more importantly, of life, begins with understanding the requirements of commitment to relationships, spiritual, family, business. Requirements are the benchmarks or milestones on the highway of accomplishment; they provide the road map for any venture. From the beginning of time, some people have tried to march to a different drummer, only to find themselves conforming to another set of requirements, ones that take them further away from their goals.

In business, we generally do a pitiful job of indoctrinating new employees, a worse job integrating them into their work assignment. Employees cry out constantly, "We don't know what's expected of us," or, "This isn't what I thought I'd be doing." If they don't understand their mission, how can they be held accountable?

Managers fail all too often because they were hired on the assumption that, as they came from a successful position, they will "hit the ground running" and somehow magically assume the reins for their department and turn it into a huge success overnight. Hyatt and Gottlieb state clearly in their book, *When Smart People Fail*, that in most situations that don't work out, the problem has to do with people misunderstanding what they were hired for.

Lack of accountability leads to the "it's not my problem" syndrome. The loss of expectations due to unaccountability was evidenced recently when the governors of several states decried the administration's effort to shift the responsibility for $21 billion to the states. If the governors and state officials had to establish requirements for spending those tax dollars, who would they have to blame when something went wrong? It's apparent in the corporate setting, as well, that when measurable assignments are handed out, many people are hiding behind the door!

It's incredible the ends people will go to in order not to be measured, when achieving goals is the only source of true happiness, satisfaction, growth and psychic income.

Some managers would rather make ethereal long-term plans, forecasts, prognostications, none of which can be measured, but are safe. With all the white-knuckling going on today due to economic cutbacks, playing it safe has become the goal far too often.

We should be doing exactly the opposite! We must get up and take action, start looking for ways to be measured, make things happen. To achieve true quality, measure customer satisfaction, and then measure every function of the organization to ensure that satisfaction is paramount. Get close to your customers; let them tell you what they want and, hence, what your planning should be. That's where the only real requirements come from. When you know them, write them on people's foreheads and verify it regularly. What gets measured gets done, and it begins at the top with senior executives who must accept accountability and demand it of others by providing clear and reasonable requirements and constant and unambiguous measurements.

IS IT WORTH IT?

Some executives think that improving quality by these slow and, sometimes painful, methods is not worthwhile. But we've seen the results on the bottom line too often to be misled by that argument. Heraclitus, back in 450 B.C. said, "There is nothing permanent except change." The world will change whether we do anything or not; but if we fail to keep up, it's certain we won't reap the profits of those who do.

In your personal life, you change too. A baby only wants instant gratification: feed me, change me, hold me. But a toddler wants to explore, preferably alone. A school child wants to learn (at least we hope he does); and a young man or woman wants love and romance. Eventually, most people want to settle down, raise a family, have a home, enjoy a hobby, save for retirement. Finally, a person realizes life is very short and he wonders what kind of imprint he made on the world. Did he click the dial toward excellence?

Doing it right the first time is more than a work ethic; it's a life ethic as well. When you go to that great executive board room in the sky, will you be proud of what you accomplished not only in business, but in your personal life? You can't really enjoy life if you're two different people. If you're a tyrant in the office, you're not going to turn around and be a loving husband and father at home. People who try it end up with drinking or drug problems, or wearing white jackets with long arms.

Tom Flood, executive vice president of Miami's Capital Bank, offers a glimpse of the ethical, purposeful, real executive. Tom says one of his life goals is to be the same person no matter where he is (situational) or who he's with: family, co-workers, customers, priest, strangers, or the homeless (whom he and his lovely wife

Sarah spend much time helping). It's easy to see the quality in Tom Flood. He's easy to work with and to love.

Everyone has a different definition of happiness; but basically they boil down to one thing: satisfaction. Just as a customer wants to be satisfied with the product or service your company provides, you, too, want to feel satisfied. Someone once said, "Love is a satisfactory sense of someone," which I think is one of the best definitions of love I've ever heard. Present satisfaction can frequently be found in having financial security, a loving relationship, and good health. But when you question elderly people who've lived through most of their lives, many of them say that they're satisfied if they can look back and think they did their best, that they made a difference, that they feel good about the result of all those hours and minutes.

That's psychic income. That's quality.

INTERVIEW with COAST INDEX COMPANY

Harry Ruotsala is a man who believes in quality. People like Harry walk what they talk. When they lay it down at the end of their lives they can feel good about themselves.

Harry was working for Hughes Aircraft Company, but wanted to start his own business. A cousin suggested making custom index tabs and he investigated the product and, after determining it could be successful, purchased the necessary equipment and rented a building. He started his company with three employees (all relatives) in 1981 and began to call on brokers who dealt in binders and index tabs. He recalls, with chagrin, that on his very first order, they made a spelling error and he had to call up the customer and apologize and do the job over.

By 1986 there were forty-five employees. Always a compassionate and forward-looking man, he provided excellent benefits in addition to good pay, and wanted to institute pension and profit-sharing plans. However, although the company was growing and making money, there were quality problems which kept profits lower than he felt they should be. They still had to do a lot of things over again.

Being so intimately involved in the daily operations, Harry was able to catch a lot of errors before they hit the production floor, and he established a rule that—unless an order were truly rush—it could not be verbal; it had to be in writing. But as the number of employees grew, others had to be depended on to catch errors. When asked about mistakes, workers would say things like, "I did the best I could." They were in a hurry to get the order out and often didn't take time to proofread. Something was missing. People didn't seem to know how to do quality and this frustrated him.

Bob Sherer had known Harry for twenty years when he started Quality Concepts. Since they were friends, Bob confided his ideas and programs to Harry and then asked if he'd be willing to let him test his theories on Coast Index employees.

Harry was a little apprehensive at first, because neither of them really knew what direction the workshops would take nor the result. But he approved the experiment. Bob wanted only ten or fifteen employees in a "class," so he came back twice more, each time becoming more confident he was on the right track. And he learned something too: learned that management had to get the same message. In fact, the employees became very attentive when their bosses sat in too. The kid in the mail room said, "Gee, I'm going to the same class the old man is," and he started to believe. The managers got an additional workshop of their own.

Harry says, "Almost immediately, the number of what we call 'redos' and 'make-overs' dropped significantly. We didn't keep track, in the old days, of what 'doing it over again' was really costing us, but we did notice that company profits increased 15 to 20 percent the first year of Bob's workshops. To be honest, quality dropped off a little, and makeovers increased slightly about three to four months after that; so we *called him in to do it again. I guess it's what Bob means when he says quality is a process, not a program. In the meantime we had lost a few employees and gained some others, so some were hearing the message for the first time. Bob comes back to our plant periodically just to walk through and talk to people and he's become a good friend to them. His appearance on the shop floor alone seems to improve work quality.*

"The most significant thing to me was that, as a result of Quality Concepts, we began to identify problem areas. The employees themselves were able to understand that they could perform better if they understood the requirements of any particular job. It improved the way they looked at things.

"You know, most people are never trained in quality work; no one teaches it in our educational system. I began to realize that we can't expect quality work from people who've never been trained, and that one of the best investments a company can make is to take the time to tell them what's required. If they meet the requirements, they're doing a quality job. I think the employees were looking for something like that. Now we're down to about 1 percent reworks. We also maintain a suggestion box and encourage employees to suggest ways of improving the product and the process. If we implement a suggestion, the employee gets recognition and a monetary gift.

"We learned to measure errors and find out how much the mistakes cost, and we share this information with employees at meetings every month or two. If you mess up a ten thousand dollar job, you have to sell a hundred thousand dollars worth of product to make up for it. We talk about the importance of profits for the company; because, without profits, there's no job longevity, no wage increases, extra benefits. We talked about workmen's compensation and how a recent case cost us fifty-five thousand dollars. That amounts to a 3 to 4 percent raise for employees, so they begin to realize it's important to prevent accidents on the job.

"We also made improvements in our hiring practices. We're over 100 employees, expanded our probationary period

from thirty days to three months, and we do a better job of screening employees on the front end. As a result, we have much lower turnover. In fact, people come to us and ask for a job because we're beginning to be seen as a quality house in the industry."

Challenge: How will you promote Doing It Right the First Time in your organization?

_____

_____

_____

_____

_____

_____

_____

_____

_____

_____

_____

12

YOU ARE WHO YOU HIRE

Tell me who your friends are and I'll tell you who you are.
Everybody's Grandmother

W hen I was with A-M, there was a program which recognized the efforts of employees to bring new recruits into the company. It was called the Talent Scout Award, and I'm proud to say I have several of those plaques. It reads, "...in recognition of his contribution to the successful growth of the A-M Sales Organization by attracting new men to the business and who, by so doing, has demonstrated his trust in the future of his company."

It sounds good, doesn't it? People who already worked for the company, and were enthusiastic enough about it to recommend it to their friends, thereby not only relieved Personnel from having to find compatible workers, and assured them of more of the kind they had already hired, but strengthened teamwork. Although it continues to work, today the practice is frowned on as being discriminatory. Another reason, perhaps, that we can't compete with the Japanese.

THE HIRING TRIGGER

The success or failure of a company is determined by many factors, both internal and external. The problems within a company may seem less threatening than external factors, because we think of them as relatively controllable. However, these internal affairs require as much careful planning and purposeful action as any marketing strategy. Creating a winning team often requires hiring new players. Getting and keeping good employees is our country's number one labor problem. Now, as America edges closer toward a complete service-based economy, employees are a company's single most important asset. Putting an emphasis on hiring the right people the first time becomes even more critical.

My daughter graduated from U.C. Davis as a nutritional therapist and she's really into the health picture. Some time ago, during a visit, we were discussing this subject and she came up with the old saw, "You are what you eat." And, in my case, she said, "Dad, you are how much you eat!"

Later I was thinking about the fact that studies have shown that healthy employees are more effective and productive than those who don't pay much attention to their diet and physical well-being. Thinking about how management attracts and retains quality employees made me suddenly think, "You are who you hire!" The people you have in the field representing you, those on the floor developing the product and the support staff are all people who speak volumes about you as the leader or manager of your group, your division, your company.

With this in mind, it's difficult to imagine the following comment, yet we hear it far too often: "How come we can't get any decent people? These people out here are no good and I can't seem to get them to do quality work." It speaks to the issue of what management is really all about: the ability to attract, hire, train and develop employees who can get and keep customers by offering quality products or services. The executive who allows an inferior work force to control the company's destiny should be aware that no one in the organization is more responsible for the employees than he. It rests with senior executives to develop a family of quality individuals dedicated to profitability through customer satisfaction.

All hands must understand where the company is going and know they are an integral part of accomplishing those goals. If you have people reporting to you, whether you're the local weekly newspaper, bank or blivet factory, you will find *you are who you hire*—and keep—and the results will tell on the bottom line.

In the current service-based climate, a company's "family of employees" will make or break the business. Unfortunately, at the very time when companies need employees who know how to work, candidates who demonstrate the potential for becoming good employees are harder than ever to find.

Advertising and placement agencies for new hire candidates are expensive. Meanwhile, customers suffer with new employees who, in many instances, *they* have to train to read and write. Competition, of course, rolls on.

LABOR IN THE '90'S

Attracting, hiring and retaining employees who understand what work is, are success oriented and highly motivated, is becoming more and more of a problem for American companies. More mistakes are committed in the selection and utilization of employees than in any other area.

The desire to develop leaders, not leaners, is the beginning of a new success culture within some companies today. Yet, too many managers' busy schedules contribute to an attitude which makes it easy to relinquish the responsibility of selecting high-performing employees. When the stack of resumes grows and the interviews seem endless, it becomes more and more attractive to leave the recruitment and screening to others, to simply hire the person Human Resources recommends. However, finding above-average employees will multiply your power, your prestige, your company's profits and productivity and yes, even your own income.

People are the heart of any business; and the wrong people, or the right people in the wrong positions, can lead to a "corporate heart attack." The objective should be to reach for the strongest person. Set your standards high. You can always reduce them; it's much harder to raise them. If you don't begin with high objectives and set your sights for above-average employees, you're not likely to attract them. Remember an empty house is better than a poor tenant.

Some managers think they're not required to attract new employees; they're convinced that all attraction takes place in the original recruitment arena, such as the recruitment tables on campuses, career days in cities, and mailings to schools. These activities will draw likely prospects, but it's up to the managers to evaluate their competence and style and determine their compatibility with the organization.

The first step for a manager to take is to prepare detailed specifications for the position. More important than the compensation issue, he should review the title, specific responsibilities, and human relationships involved, as well as the experience and education required. Prospective employees must feel good not only about the position and the company, but about how they will relate to the company. To do a good job of recruitment, interviewing managers must share the company's vision, strategy and excitement for the future or the high-performing candidate will not be interested.

During multiple interviews, the successful manager must explain the position's significance to the company's total mission and stress the uniqueness and potential for contribution that this particular position can bring to the company.

The weighing of a candidate's personal qualities needs to be a more thoughtful and lengthy procedure than the gut reaction which usually occurs in the first few minutes of an interview. Managers should not make snap judgments, but should decide by observation and discussion, whether an individual possesses the traits necessary for success in a particular position. Successful leaders understand that appropriately matching employees to positions will ultimately lead to greater profits and growth.

Well-qualified candidates are aggressively pursued by other companies as well, so, once again, managers must share the company's vision and strategy, as well as the career path. The manager must make the candidate *want* to join the company.

The successful manager must be a leader and a mentor and demonstrate an ongoing concern for the employee to become acclimated and successful. Regardless of whether it's a person's first job, or later in his career, managers should understand the critical nature of hiring for success.

One organization we know tracks new hires by manager to determine the manager's success in choosing quality employees. This becomes an important measurement for evaluating the performance of the manager. To qualify for promotion or greater span of control, a manager needs to demonstrate the ability to strengthen the company by adding valuable employees.

We have a responsibility to new managers *prior* to their first management assignment, to train and help them understand the importance to the company—and moreover to their future promotions—of the need to attract and hire excellent people.

Making an investment to set up a tracking procedure that assures that managers value their hiring record will reduce the expense of turnover and guarantee the strength of the company's greatest asset: its *people*!

FIVE COMPONENTS OF HIRING

There are a lot of people out of work, yet isn't it interesting that quality employees are always in demand and never have a problem finding opportunities?

Effective leaders know that the competition for new talent will be as stringent as it is for new clients. When an advertisement is placed today, if it's answered, who shows up? There are search firms who are so starved for new candidates that they end up rotating the same crop as often as they can get away with it.

Some people in the employment agency business earn the handle "headhunter" because, in addition to rotating applicants, they may—while working to find someone for us—at the same time try to recruit us for another company. Fortunately, there are a few well-respected search companies and they're rated at the top of the field. Honesty, integrity, dignity and moral ethics keep them in demand.

Managers must understand that the job of proper staffing of the organization is made up of five parts: attracting, hiring, training, promoting and terminating.

The first is attraction. In order to find talent, you must create a situation or environment where prospective winners want to work. This sounds like "Which comes first, the chicken or the egg?" in order to get quality employees you must have a quality environment; and in order to have a quality environment, you must have quality employees. If you're just beginning to turn your company around, to make an all-out effort to provide quality products and services to your customers, you may not yet have all the pieces in place. Yet, when you recruit people, you articulate your vision for the future of the company—for instilling quality procedures—and how each member will benefit from being part of the team.

The smart leader always has a "bench" back-up just in case someone leaves or gets hit by a bus. A good team depends on a leader who is always scouting for champions.

Hiring is the second piece of building a new team talent. Who are you getting? One fellow I know visits the prospective employee's home at dinner time (with a valid question about the application). He learns more from this visit than all the interviews possible. Is it worth it? You bet. He sees how they live and that's how they'll work once they're on board. Is it legal? Sure. Your concern is creating a quality climate for the sake of other employees, It's not only fair to find out as much as you can about the new prospect, its's your responsibility.

Prior to "pulling the hiring trigger," management should commit to attracting and finding the best people and then be sure they are what they seem to be. Peel them down by any legal and ethical means at your disposal. It should be an accepted norm that hitting the bull's-eye will provide long term benefits. Devoted employees, and a work force all pulling in the same direction, bring profits.

HIRING FOR PROFIT

News of corporate mergers and acquisitions dominate the business world, and a manager should consider that hiring a new employee is a merger too. Companies spend millions of dollars a year on information to insure the development of a profitable team; why not spend half an hour of your interview time to make sure that the person you interview and the person you hire are really one and the same?

To clarify this statement, understand that what you see during the interview is usually not what you get once you've hired that person. When schools lost the focus of teaching reading, writing and arithmetic many years ago, they started teaching the fine art of interviewing, and most job candidates have been schooled in resume writing and interviewing techniques in class and from a glut of books on the subject. In Interview 101, they learn how to write a resume, what to wear, what to say, and the *right* answers to questions. From the street corner, to the MBA mills, the latest scoop on how to "impress for success" is easily available. So when the interviewee shows up, how do you find the real person?

The successful manager hiring for profit must also have some tools to unmask the impostor and discover the truly motivated employee interested in merging his skills with those of the company team. One piece of hiring is checking out references and history. It never ceases to amaze me when companies find out that employees are not as proficient or skilled as their applications claimed. Often previous jobs are invented, as bold applicants suspect little checking will be done. This is largely due to government regulations and a legal society that has previous employers concerned enough about lawsuits that they pass on virtually no information about previous employees.

I once hired a bright, shiny, young all-American type based solely on looks and a lunch. Within 30 days the fellow disappeared and evidence came to light that he was a fugitive, wanted in three states. This is called a *real* learning experience. A little checking in front pays big dividends, yet we're always in a hurry, looking for shortcuts.

How is it that some people end up in jobs that are totally foreign to their natures? I've seen a personnel manager who flatly admitted, "I hate people." And you've no doubt come across many a sales person who ought to have been raising rabbits for a living instead of dealing with customers.

During a series of workshops we gave to a very large American corporation, we asked executives to rank a list of values in order of importance to their organization. The Human Resources Manager was shocked to discover, at the end of the exercise, that the items he had put at the bottom of his list were the very ones that the company's employees put at the top of theirs, items such as "support" and "appreciation."

In his article, "Job Interviews—from Your Side of the Desk," in *CBT Directions*, personnel manager Donald G. Smith says intelligence is one of the vital things he looks for in a candidate. When traced to the source, bad decisions are almost always made by people who aren't very bright, he finds, but intelligent people adapt easily and learn their jobs quickly. They also understand their assignments, and can see beyond immediate results into the future. "Like cream, intelligence and stupidity rise to the top in a matter of minutes and present themselves for inspection" during an interview, Smith says.

Nevertheless, it's easy to find yourself trapped in a Jekyll and Hyde situation when hiring a new employee. Even if the candidate doesn't list "Member of Mensa" (the organization for people who score in the top two percent on standard I.Q. tests) on his resume, you can determine the level of intelligence if you invest the time to do so. Brilliant people, however, may not always get along with others and fit well in the organization, so additional interviews with different levels of employees should take place. When employees accept a candidate they will help make the new hire successful.

Many years ago, I discovered a hiring technique that often allowed me to identify the real person I was interviewing. My technique is simple. During the interview I try both to disarm the candidate and to discover if he is someone interested in the company. First I relax and allow him to demonstrate if he has learned something about the business beforehand. If not, does he ask questions about the company? My next step is to remove the parameters of the normal job interview. I announce, for example, that I have something to pick up at the hardware store, and since it's only a block or two away, would he mind walking with me while we continue our interview? Someone educated in the standard responses to a job interview will become flustered. But, I've had every response, from disbelief, to enthusiastic agreement. Once out of the office, the interview environment becomes completely different. The candidate's questions range from, "What are we looking for?" or, "How long will this take?" to, "Who's your favorite team, etc.?" By the time we've reached the store, I'm able to determine whether this person has any motivation; whether, in other words, I will be hiring for profit.

Once inside the store, the candidate is either standing at the entrance watching me wander up and down the aisles, glancing at his watch, or wandering along with me, slightly amused, or is two or three aisles away, holding up a screwdriver and shouting, "Is this what you're looking for?"

My technique is simple, effective and to the point. If there isn't a hardware store near by, consider inviting your prospective employee to a meeting or the company picnic, as Paul Hawkins suggested in his 1987 book, *Growing a Business*. The goal is to remove the individual from her role style. But interviewing is only the first step in hiring for profit. The successful manager must also be interested in ensuring that, once hired, the new employee becomes properly integrated into the new working environment. Training the new hire is a lost art in American business. Too many managers are either buried in work that is easily delegated to team members, or use their workload as an excuse to avoid spending the necessary time in the selection and training process. The successful manager hiring for profit must understand the necessity of hiring the right person. And for a successful employment merger to take place, the integration process must be continued long after that initial trip to the hardware store.

PUPPY PHILOSOPHY

Way back in my days in San Jose I had to add people to the sales force. Sometimes the applicant looked so good, I came to wonder, "If this candidate is so great, how come I'm the lucky one to get him?" It's when I developed my Puppy Philosophy.

Some firms like to hire people with degrees. Others like to hire people with experience. To use their expression, they like a person, "who can hit the ground running," someone already in the marketplace. "We don't have time to train people," they say. That's a cop-out! If these experienced people are so good, why are they available? If they're so good, why are they leaving their present job? When I worked for a major corporation, and we hired someone that great, we often found there was something odd about these "miracle" candidates. Strangely, they never seemed to work out.

This is not to say *no* qualified, experienced candidates should be hired. Some are available because their former employer went out of business, or the company was merged or moved to a new location, or they found themselves at odds with the philosophy of the company, or maybe you made them an offer they couldn't refuse. The point is that you must check out the reasons, to the greatest extent possible, before hiring someone who sounds "too good to be true." They usually are.

My philosophy is that you can sometimes find a bright young person who is eager, just like a puppy. And you raise him and train him, teach him your products and your company philosophy. A couple of ounces of desire are sometimes better than pounds of experience and a degree.

People who come out of college with degrees and fall right into management jobs know virtually nothing of practical value. If they've never made a payroll and worked in the job market, they've never earned their way. Conrad Hilton put his executives in the lowliest jobs in his hotels from time to time, to learn. When, at A-M, I was faced with these "instant managers," and saw their lack of knowledge and experience, I often said, "Why don't you go out and travel with the guys on the street? Talk to customers; get in the trenches. The employees will respect you for it and you'll know what's happening." But they wouldn't do that. That's one of the reasons the company filed for bankruptcy.

THE ON-BOARD TERRORIST

In some companies, the shortage of workers has led to adopting some version of the old A-M Talent Scout Program. It can succeed today if this activity is coupled with a fair policy toward all comers, and will survive government scrutiny. Whatever methodology you use, there is always a danger that you may, inadvertently, hire an "on-board terrorist."

If there's an employee in your company who does shoddy work, fails to observe directions, and tries to lure other workers into his disruptive methods, you have an on-board terrorist. Hopefully, you won't allow such a person to recommend another employee, for it's pretty obvious he'd be likely to suggest someone like himself, thereby doubling your quota of internal enemies.

How *do* you get rid of terrorists? Firing is the obvious answer; but today government regulations can make that extremely difficult. You have to document your efforts to correct the employee, keep specific records of non-compliance, and sometimes deal with a union besides. Some managers simply throw up their hands and try to keep the terrorist's damage to a minimum. This is a company killer.

In companies where managers have devoted enough time to attract and select quality employees, terrorists don't get a foothold to begin with; but if they do show up, excellent managers sometimes find that the other employees—the good ones who have been carefully selected and properly trained—will gradually force out the terrorist. They let him know they're not interested in stealing time by excessive conversation or too-long lunch breaks. As internal customers they complain if the terrorist doesn't pass along quality work. And they shun someone who violates the rules about alcohol on the job, or uses drugs. In many of the divisions I took over during my years in the corporate world, some employees left because they felt uncomfortable; they knew they didn't fit into the new environment I was creating.

A client company once had an on-board terrorist who was in a very important job. They couldn't just fire him. But they were putting Quality Concepts ideas to work and the other employees didn't let this man deter them from moving in the right direction. Finally I had a telephone call from the company president. He said, "I have good news: Our OBT has quit!" I said, "That's great!" and he said, "No, that's not the good news; the good news is that he went to work for our competitor!"

It's very important to realize that on-board terrorists don't always start out that way. Sometimes they have problems: alcohol, a disintegrating marriage, a sick child; sometimes they need help. When a company has shifted, employees may find themselves fearful and alone. Management must recognize the reasons behind their behavior, and provide some solutions. It may be able to turn them around and make them productive members of the team.

TURNOVER

Employees come and go; that's a fact of life. Turnover and retraining eat up profits left and right. Be certain you don't add to the problem with bad hires. Selecting the wrong employee or putting an individual in the wrong position just results in increased turnover and all of the attendant costs.

It's extraordinary to see the level of turnover in some companies while some senior managers apparently remain oblivious to the direct link between high turnover and its negative impact on customers, which leads to dwindling profits. Recently the American Banking Association released figures that indicated the replacement cost of a bank teller is in excess of five thousand dollars and that of a mid-level manager is in excess of forty thousand. These numbers are staggering; so imagine the cost to those banks whose turnover reaches 25 to 50 percent a year.

What's a reasonable turnover rate? Every company is different; yet there should be enough to allow new talent to come aboard without disruption.

Turnover is costly. Besides the investment in advertising, recruiting, interviewing and training, many firms pick up the cost of moving a family and pay for interim housing, real estate fees and other incidentals. This says nothing about the first months of acclimation, when there is little or no productivity. If there's a lot of this going on at your company, you're running hard just to stand still.

One of the hidden costs of heavy turnover is the lowering of morale of the remaining workers. Suddenly, their work load increases to make up for the missing person. They can get burned out, make costly errors, or become candidates for resignation themselves, thereby exacerbating the situation.

One major reason for turnover is incompatible social and interpersonal skills. Surveys show that a great percentage of turnover results, not from lack of technical skills, but from inability to get along with others. Therefore, a strong case is made for training managers to learn how to identify candidates who exhibit the proper skills and attitudes and understand the appropriate match-ups that affect profits and growth.

Some industries have higher turnover rates than others. In the service sector in particular, where skills mainly pertain to specialized knowledge or the ability to sell a product—any product—people can be harder to hold onto. This often leaves managers with a fatalistic attitude. They come to believe that all workers are greedy, that any worker will desert the ship if he can get a better salary or more benefits elsewhere. Yet, there's a company in Boston that, although it pays very well, has a 30 percent turnover rate. One former worker was quoted as saying, "People even took pay cuts to get out of there."

On the other hand, a large number of firms keep their staff, not with huge salaries and perks, but by building teams, caring about their people and playing fair. To a skilled observer, it's obvious that lack of leadership is the culprit when turnover is excessive; and owners who fail to correct the situation are buying problems for the future.

DEVELOPING PEOPLE

Andrall E. Pearson, writing in the *Harvard Business Review*, reminds executives they must maintain consistent, demanding standards for everyone in the company, beginning with hiring practices that upgrade the quality, rather than just fill vacancies. The executive must be able to recognize high potential in managers and develop them quickly, to rotate "promising people carefully to expose them to different problems and functions."

"...traditional approaches to people development—like promotion from within based chiefly on job tenure—are no longer good enough," says Pearson. "A company that uses experience as its primary criterion for advancement is encouraging organizational hardening of the arteries..." He believes that "...mergers and acquisitions, new technology, price pressures and the information explosion all require a stronger and more savvy management team, people who can innovate and win in an uncertain future."

Yet, the shrinking numbers of new recruits—and the fact that many of the brightest head for Wall Street, consulting and entrepreneurship—makes this more difficult than ever. Advancing technology may mean retraining some employees in new skills; and it's often cheaper than hiring. In one company, management learned that retraining an engineer was less than one-third of the cost of hiring a new one.

One way to be sure to have the right people when you need them is to hire them when you don't! To have talented people in a crisis may mean hiring good ones whenever you find them—and to be constantly on the lookout—even if you have no specific job for them at the moment. While waiting for the right slot to drop them into, these recruits can be employed on special projects, or shifted around to learn about different facets of the business. This is a scheme that Pearson used at PepsiCo and which proved highly successful.

This method of hiring sounds expensive, but it's often cheaper than bringing in consultants when an emergency occurs and push comes to shove.

In the retail business, hiring the wrong people is not just unprofitable; it can be disastrous.

I was shopping in a department store one day and received very poor service. Finally I went to their office to complain and was told they were sorry but they were doing their best.

"What about Nordstrom?" I asked.

"They give good service." The manager answered, "But they hire better people."

"How can that be?" I said. "They're in the same shopping mall. They use the same employee pool that you do."

"They pay more," she admitted.

"Why is that?"

"They make more money."

I rest my case.

Challenge: What will you do to attract and hire the right people for your organization?

_____

_____

_____

_____

_____

_____

_____

_____

_____

_____

_____

_____

_____

_____

TRAINING THE TROOPS

13

To teach is to learn.
Japanese Proverb

I n Tokyo, in 1979, Konosuke Matsushita, Executive Director of Matsushita Electric Industrial Co., Ltd. said this about western industrialized nations:

"We are going to win and the industrial West is going to lose out. There's nothing much you can do about it, because the reasons for your failure are within yourselves... For us, the core of management is the art of mobilizing and pulling together the intellectual resources of all employees in the service of the firm... This is why our large companies give their employees three to four times more training than yours."

TRAINING

Every company with a quality-improvement process in place says, "You can't do too much training." Yet far too many companies profess to believe that employees are their greatest asset while at the same time straining—rather than training—them with poor directions, lack of leadership and expanded workloads. The strategy of "lean and mean" is often what the phrase implies: a very lean investment in employees and a very mean style of management which fails to understand the real motivating factors that produce employees who will go the extra mile for the company and the customers.

An organization can become lean by reducing the number of benefit-eligible workers, and certainly benefits are a major cost today; yet what is the cost to customers, internal as well as external, faced with part-time workers who've been given little or no training? How can you build a team if part-time employees, who work four hours a day, many of whom may not have been in the work force for years and have no experience with recent technological changes, are expected to interface with full-time employees?

This is not to say that part time help is a bad idea. It's a great idea if the organization is willing to make the investment in these people. As the available pool of quality candidates shrinks, utilizing those who want only to, or must, work short hours may become a necessity. High-performing students, and parents who want to be home when their children return from school, will be needed if some companies are to keep a work force in place.

Some executives, studying the successful Japanese organizations, have discovered that where American companies have 12 to 14 managers between the senior and supervisory levels, Toyota has four. Consequently, they see this as a way to save money by eliminating executive positions. This is a healthy move, but only if the training of those left in place is sufficient to enable them to carry out their responsibilities. Unfortunately, there's little evidence to show that many companies are offering this training. Employees who are led by untrained supervisors, and managers who are frustrated by their inability to do their jobs, are both candidates for switching careers. Such high turnover reflects directly on the bottom line, and results in still more belt-tightening as senior management tries to solve the problem.

Writing in the March, 1996, *Money* Magazine, Managing Editor Frank Lalli says, "Here's a stock tip: investors should stop chasing after companies that are saving money by laying off workers and start switching to firms that spend money training their employees. The payoff may not be instantly obvious. At least, it's certainly eluded Wall Street, which continues to pump up the share prices of any corporation with a CEO who can spell 'downsize.' For example, AT&T's stock rose $2.50 a share when the company announced its intention to discard 40,000 employees. Fact is, layoffs often just misleadingly inflate the company's reported profits, while diverting management attention from solving the underlying problems..."

For investors, the message is revealed in a seven-year study of 25 large corporations. A 30 percent reduction in employment caused only an average 1.5 percent reduction in operating costs. In addition, although the downsizing caused its stock to rise initially, after three years, it was up less than 5 percent; whereas companies which didn't reduce employment as heavily enjoyed increases of more than 30 percent.

This was echoed by a top Labor Department official who said that "something is out of whack" when private pension funds use the employees' savings to buy stock in companies that throw other employees out of work.

However, for leaders who feel the necessity to downsize, another survey of 1003 large and medium-sized corporations shows that those reporting layoffs, *while at the same time increasing the training they gave their workers*, were more than twice as likely to enjoy increased productivity, and therefore profits, than those which didn't.

Labor Secretary Robert Reich has proposed granting an income tax reduction to companies which significantly increase their expenditures for employee retraining, believing that a slight loss in taxes now may mean more taxes paid later as workers learn new skills.

Training is important at Federal Express. All new managers attend the Leadership Institute for 13 weeks; and continuing education for all managers is provided by the Quality Academy. All employees, once a year, fill out a confidential opinion survey which rates their manager, their manager's manager, and the company. This process is known as SFA, Survey Feedback Action. Each level surveyed has a three-week period in which to develop a plan to deal with employee feedback and must report what they're going to do to correct any deficiencies.

Another winning strategy is their "people first" policy. They promote from within, promise no layoffs, constantly communicate, and give their people the tools to do their jobs. One of these tools is the power to deliver exceptional customer service. Their couriers can send flowers or candy to customers, or even refund up to $100 if a delivery is late. Their attrition rate is about one percent a year. It's not surprising then, that they were awarded the Malcolm Baldrige National Quality Award, the first service company to win.

Each of us who runs a company or a department must ask ourselves, "What kind of training do we provide?" Make a list of these programs. Then ask, "What additional training should we be doing?" Involve your employees, by utilizing them as trainers. They know the important aspects of training to focus on. They learn by teaching and that builds confidence.

The information in the following chart, taken from *Fortune* Magazine, shows the training commitment of several successful companies.

COMPANY EMPLOYEES	TRAINING	
	PERCENT OF PAY-ROLL SPENT IN 1992	AVG HRS PER EM-PLOYEE PER YEAR
Motorola 107,000	3.6%	36
Federal Express 93,000	4.5%	27
Andersen Consulting 26,700	6.8%	109
Corning 14,000 (dom)	3.0%	92
Solectron 3,500	3.0%	95
Dudek Mfgng. 35	5.0%	25

Today we're faced with a level of competition, coupled with a work force that is extraordinarily expensive and less productive, that is unmatched by anything in our past. Consequently, management, to a great degree, is frustrated, and we often react to frustration with anger and lash out at the very thing that we should be ennobling, mentoring, and nurturing: the employees who will either sink the ship by drilling a hole in the bottom or put us over the top and carry the coach off the field when they win the Super Bowl of customer satisfaction.

Is it surprising that we have management that doesn't know how to treat employees? It shouldn't be. We have parents who don't know how to treat children. If you tell children, or employees, that they're dumb or stupid or useless, you can just about guarantee that's what they'll become. And some managers treat their employees in this fashion as a daily occurrence.

Today, when worthwhile employees can pick and choose who they'll work for, a style of management that intimidates them, beats them down or fails to give them the tools with which to do their job, can't long endure. This doesn't mean that management must be "wimpy" or soft; the policies of Nordstrom, Federal Express and Wal-Mart are anything but that; but they protect their employees and satisfied employees equals satisfied customers.

Why doesn't everyone do it? Because it isn't easy. It requires true commitment and dedication from the most senior level of management.

TURNING THINGS AROUND

How can management deal with this opportunity? To begin with, by demonstrating that employees are the most important asset the company has. This instills pride in the employee, and gives meaningful purpose to each job. Unfortunately, this is difficult for many executives; trusting those people in peer or subordinate positions does not come easily and is not taught in the institutions of higher learning.

Management training must focus in part on managers learning to trust their people. Employees must be convinced that *they* are the company, and that *their* success will ensure the success of the company.

Every executive needs to determine how to make each employee more successful in his individual job. Too many times the vital first few days of an employee's indoctrination consists merely of leafing through an employee manual and a cursory review of company do's and don'ts. Instead, the indoctrination ought to include teaching new employees what is expected of them, what is the global view of the company as to the quality of the product or service they offer, and the significance of their piece of the action. If you've heard the remarks, "Don't ask me, I just work here," or, "That's not my job," you can almost bet it came from the lack of a thorough indoctrination about the company goals and how to play a dedicated role in achieving them, not just for company profitability but for their own personal sense of accomplishment and pride.

Communication is the vital link. Continue to ask them what they think. Listen. Employ their ideas when possible. Let the employees know you consider them to be *your* customers. Give them the products, tools and encouragement and amazing things will happen.

I repeat: it's not easy. Yet of what worth is "easy" if your service status quo is the customer's woe? This is not an experiment; it's a culture change that must be communicated in certain undeniable, concrete terms of commitment. The fun and success of profits and satisfied customers will last long after the pain of changing management philosophy has been forgotten.

ADVERSARIES

One of the reasons leaders value a candidate's personality more than any other quality is because dealing with personality conflicts among his staff can use up a great deal of time, and productivity suffers as a result. Communicating a team culture eliminates many of these problems.

Employees who have no real commitment to a company sabotage it in subtle and not so subtle ways. Time theft, for example, can amount to as much as four and a half hours a week, or six weeks out of a year, according to a survey by Robert Half International. Employees who arrive late to work, or leave early, take long breaks or lunch hours, feign illness, or perform personal (or even moonlighting) tasks in the shop or office on company time are invariably those who feel remote from their managers and from the culture of the firm.

To be fair, hourly workers aren't the only ones stealing time from their employers. Managers waste four weeks a year looking for misplaced items, according to another survey, and three weeks a year making unnecessary telephone calls.

The traditional method of combating these unpleasant statistics has been to tighten controls. Managers then spend much of their time patrolling the workers, observing them to make sure they're on the job, reprimanding them when violations are found, and generally reinforcing the feeling among the work force that management is "them," and labor is "us." Or vice versa. It always amazed me that a company could expect to survive, let alone prosper, when union and management fought one another, often during a long and bitter strike, and then, when the dust of battle cleared, expect to work together in harmony until the next contract negotiation.

America can no longer afford that kind of adversarial relationship. Instead, we must embrace and develop methods for the future.

Frederick Reichheld is the author of *the Loyalty Effect, The Hidden Force Behind Growth, Profits, and Lasting Value,* published in 1996 by the Harvard Business School Press. In it, Reichheld says that, instead of downsizing, employers should focus directly on involving their employees in value and loyalty to the company's philosophy.

"Businesses need employees who are loyal to the idea of creating great value for customers, so much value that there is enough left over to reward employees and investors," he said in an interview.

Reichheld's book is the result of long-term studies of successful and unsuccessful companies, and he maintains that a focus on loyalty creates not only productive employees, but satisfied customers as well. He believes that today's focus on accounting is a short-term one that will lead to eventual loss of value and customers. Business leaders need to ask themselves, "What is in our customers' best interests?"

Loyalty used to be considered the attitude that employees had to their employers; but Reichheld maintains that loyalty on the part of employers to their employees is a hidden force that needs to be utilized in order for profits to grow.

"Layoffs," Reichheld says, "have far more costs associated with them than most executives realize," since they almost always cause churning, an eventual dip in productivity and poorer service to customers. It's time to counter such a downward spiral with loyalty and partnership with employees and customers.

To Aaron Feuerstein, president of Malden Mills in Lawrence, Massachusetts, loyalty to workers is no more than common decency. Feuerstein, you may remember from news stories in December, 1995, is the man who, when his textile factory was nearly destroyed by fire, vowed to keep his employees on the payroll rather than laying them off.

This decision, which, in this era of corporate downsizing and "lean and mean" environment, seems Utopian, cost Feuerstein $10 million in pay and full health-care benefits for his workers.

Yet, he gained more than the feeling that he did the right thing. His loyalty to his workers has resulted in a record-breaking rebuilding of his facility (Three months later, two of the three Malden divisions were up and running at almost full capacity.) and a doubling of production, while at the same time effecting a significant drop in the number of defects in their products.

Admirers of this unusual, but heart-warming, decision have flooded the plant with thousands of letters from all over the world; and Feuerstein will be rewarded with at least five honorary degrees from American universities. Yet, he doesn't consider what he did to be praise-worthy. In an interview in the *Christian Science Monitor* in March, 1996, Feuerstein said, "There's some kind of crazy belief that if you discard the responsibility to your... workers, and think only of the immediate profit, that somehow not only your company will prosper but the entire economy will prosper as a result... And I think that's dead wrong." He said it would be extremely profitable to have taken the insurance money after the fire and not rebuilt his mills, but he was raised to do the right thing.

"What kind of an ethic is it that a CEO is prepared to hurt 3,000 people who are his employees (and) an entire city of many more thousands... in order for him to have a short-term gain.... It's unthinkable," he said.

Feuerstein, of course, has the advantage of being his own boss with no shareholders to answer to, but he feels—as do the thousands of people who have heard his story—that a moral imperative is beyond price. Furthermore, he has proved that it will bring rewards in both the short and long term.

SERVICE

Zenger-Miller, Inc, a training firm, says that American corporations spend only $2.58 per employee per year to improve their service to customers. And the greater part is for training to sell more products or handle complaints, not offer true service in the first place. Emery Air Freight recently announced a plan to spend $1,000 each to train employees in proper service; and Ryder System says it's sending all its executives to a "quality college." U.S. Sprint is actively engaged in a program to train both hourly workers and executives; but some heads of banking institutions still admit they spend less money training people who don't deal directly with the public. This is a critical mistake when we understand that every employee has an internal customer, and that not satisfying that person can ultimately lead to problems that *will* affect the external customer.

A family I know used to take the local daily newspaper which was delivered—as is usual—by a kid on a bicycle after school. They had a covered sidewalk, about 20 feet long and five feet wide, leading to their front door; and they told the carrier they would like him to throw it *anywhere* on that sidewalk, not exactly a small target. For a few days, the paper could be found there, but then it began to turn up on the driveway, under a car, or in the street. Complaints brought only excuses: "We have a new carrier," "The regular boy was out sick."

Delivery improved for a day or two after each complaint; then the paper began to show up in the bushes, up a tree or even on the roof! The husband told the customer service representative: "I used to deliver papers myself when I was a boy, and every customer wanted it in a certain convenient place. If it landed somewhere else, I had to get off my bike and pick up the paper and put it where it belonged. If not, I'd get chewed out and risk losing the job."

The company promised that the problem would never occur again. But it did almost immediately, and the family canceled its subscription.

Do you think it's impossible these days for carriers to put the newspaper in the right place? Think again. That family switched to *U.S.A. Today*, told the company where they wanted the paper delivered and for the next six years—until they moved away—the carrier hit that exact spot every day as if an "X" had been chalked there.

TRAINING SALESPEOPLE

More managers than ever these days manage sales people; and their greatest challenge is developing knowledgeable, caring associates who understand the importance of providing excellent service. Customers have many sources for their needs today; if you provide a product that can be purchased in other places, you run the risk of having customers leave for greener pastures. You must then compete on the basis of service, value, price, or convenience.

There's a limit to how low the price can drop before you go out of business. We long ago stopped laughing at the old joke, "Oh, sure, I lose money on every item, but I make it up with volume."

Sometimes we have no control over convenience. If our store is located in a shrinking neighborhood, or one with ever larger numbers of potential non-customers for our type of service, we have little choice but to move or go under. The value of our product may be superb, but if others sell the same thing, we may have no advantage. Service, then, is the separator of the winners from the losers. People like good service and are willing to pay more for it. Often however, it's not a case of providing excellent service and therefore being able to raise our prices; in today's competitive world, it may mean our very survival. Customers who enjoy shopping in a particular store or mall spend more money there and do it more often.

As a manager, you need to hold regular meetings with your staff to remind them that their job is more than selling gloves or hardware or bank loans; it's helping customers. You have to teach them what questions to ask, when to let the customer browse, when to make recommendations and to always be courteous and solicitous.

In addition, you need to assure them the customer always comes first, not stocking inventory, rearranging sales receipts or cleaning shelves. As a leader, you have the responsibility for seeing that salespeople aren't kept busy with these lateral assignments during selling hours, and that their non-customer duties are prioritized and take as little time as possible. Employees look to leaders for guidance and example. You can't inject care for customers into your sales people unless you practice it yourself.

W.I.I.F.M.

W.I.I.F.M. stands for, "What's In It For Me?" Candidates for employment today differ vastly from earlier generations. Today managers are faced with a far greater problem than just producing a product that will sell. Today management must face an issue unknown in the history of the American work force. There used to be a labor pool for businesses, so that in effect one could put up a Help Wanted sign in the window and someone qualified would show up. Today this is no longer true. Managers at all levels are frustrated with the lack of available people to keep their businesses running. McDonald's, formerly staffed entirely by teenagers, now hires retired people to fill this gap.

In their article, "Making Impossible Dreams Come True," published in *Stanford Business School Magazine*, James C. Collins and Jerry Porras introduced a catchy phrase: "Profits are peachy, but purpose is paramount." They go on to remind us that, "Profit, while not inconsistent with purpose, fails to inspire people to their highest levels of performance... Purpose is something far more enduring, powerful and inspirational."

An old, old story is told about two bricklayers working on a building. A passerby asked the first man, "What are you doing?" and he answered in a disgruntled tone, "I'm laying bricks, of course." The passerby then went to the second man and asked the same question. This bricklayer smiled and looked upward as he said, "I'm building a cathedral." Perhaps the two men did identical work, but which one do you suppose was the happiest?

If employees don't find their own motivation in their work, it's up to leaders to help them find it. One way is through recognition. Many employees feel that employers don't recognize their good work and compliment them for it. Some have switched jobs because of lack of praise for their accomplishments. In a recent survey by Motivational Systems, 38 percent of the respondents said their supervisors rarely or never praise their work. "Twenty-seven percent said they'd leave their job for a similar one at a company known for giving employees recognition."

"If praise is used correctly," said Dr. Roger Flax, president of Motivational Systems, "it not only builds trust and respect... but has a ripple effect, communicating to the group that good performance is going to be recognized and appreciated."

Many companies have struggled with the issue and a great many variations of positive strokes have been born. Some have died a necessary death. Employee of the Month, although successful at many companies, is a failure at others. In too many cases, this has turned out to be little more than a popularity contest and workers began to view the winners with suspicion. Rather than motivating people to work better, it sometimes came across as patronizing and phony. Because the best employee is usually *always* the best, the award got passed along to almost everyone who wasn't a disaster.

Awards should only be given for outstanding performance, clearly above and beyond the norm; otherwise fellow employees will become jealous or resentful, because they feel *their* contribution was as good or better.

The most effective programs are often those in which the employees themselves nominate the winners. Even then, sometimes certain individuals are chosen more than once, and leaders should find out why more workers aren't challenged to try to earn the reward.

Rich Reed, president of InData, Inc. holds monthly meetings with his employees, and has each department head present an award to someone *from outside his group* for something which he felt contributed to the benefit of his department. No one in the organization knows in advance who will be honored, and, like an Academy Awards presentation, the excitement and joy is widespread. Winners go to lunch that day with Mr. Reed.

Several of our clients reward employees by arranging visits to customers' locations. This means a trip, a couple of nice meals, and a chance to get outside and dress up for some customer recognition. These employees have said that they enjoyed being taken to see where the products they helped build are actually used, and to be told by the customers' agents how much their work was appreciated. Money has no memory, but recognition lingers.

Increasing job satisfaction and saving money go hand in hand when a company encourages suggestions from the workers. In 1990 the National Association of Suggestion Systems reported that American businesses saved two billion dollars by adopting suggestions made by employees. Although the cash rewards were appreciated, most workers claimed to be happiest over the fact that their ideas were taken seriously and used.

It takes time, but every employee should have a personal performance review by his superior more than once a year. Not just an announcement that he'll be getting a raise, it should be a time of getting to know the employee better, reviewing his successes and failures, asking for his reaction to what you're saying, and—most important—reviewing his long-term goals and future plans. If you know what skills they want to develop and where they hope to be in five or ten years, you're in a better position to move both your employees and the company closer to success.

Honor and recognition not only have a positive effect on the bottom line, they also reduce turnover, get things done right the first time more often and achieve a higher level of customer satisfaction.

EDUCATION

On-the-job training of the U.S. work force is a contributing factor—if not the most important—in providing quality products and services necessary to survive in the next decade. But, educating that same force may make the difference between America sinking and swimming in the global economy. Writing in *The Atlantic Monthly*, Robert B. Reich, Labor Secretary under President Clinton, pointed out that worldwide competition will require educating our young people in problem-solving and problem-identifying skills. "The idea of 'goods' as something distinct from 'services' has become meaningless," Reich says, "because so much of the value provided by a successful enterprise... entails services: the specialized research, engineering, design and production services necessary to solve problems; the sales, marketing and consulting services necessary to identify problems; and the strategic, financial and management services necessary to broker the first two." A tall order.

Such skills, however, don't wear out like machinery, or become depleted like resources, or expire like patents; in fact they grow stronger and more valuable with use. A work force with these skills will keep us competitive in the 21st century.

But, the foundation for these skills lies in education; and the United States is behind most of the industrialized nations in its expenditures on primary and secondary education. Just as we recognize the need for intellectual ability, we find ourselves spending less and less to bring it about.

Many states are poised to issue school vouchers for use at private or public schools, once court challenges are settled. Charter schools are taking hold. Some are run by teachers and parents or even businesses that contract with school boards to try their own approach to improve education. In the future, some public schools will be run by business, improving fiscal responsibility as well as focusing on meaningful education.

Study after study shows that higher levels of education lead to higher ultimate salaries; and, unfortunately, the gap between these groups is widening. Ten years ago, the average college graduate earned 80 percent more than the non-graduate; now it's 160 percent more! At the same time, fewer lower and middle-class families can afford to send their children to college. In addition to pushing Congress to tackle the education problem seriously, business leaders must meet the challenge personally. With the future of our nation inextricably tied to the future of business and industry, we can't afford to wait much longer.

Meanwhile, employers are faced with many poorly educated workers. Training them to do what we require of them has already expanded into teaching some of them the Three R's. It helps, even if it's just so they'll know that the letters W.O.R.K. don't stand for a radio station. Xerox Corporation has a world-class learning center in place; and Corning and Zumar are educating many of their employees as well. Quality Concepts has hired Jose Garcia, who for 20 years was a schoolteacher, to conduct learning workshops in Spanish to workers in some client companies.

Forced by the growing number of functionally-illiterate or foreign-born recruits, some firms provide in-house classes in reading and other basic school subjects, taught by certified, or retired teachers. Ford, GM, Prudential and Polaroid are just a few of the companies that provide courses in literacy.

A few firms even hold classes in etiquette: teaching their employees who must deal with the public to say "please" and "thank you," cover their mouths if they sneeze or yawn, and chew with their mouths closed. In fact, according to a recent *Newsweek* article, universities, fraternities, job-placement services and savvy entrepreneurs are conducting classes in etiquette to help employees land a job in the first place. They tell them, "If your mother didn't teach you table manners when you were six, you'd better brush up on the niceties before you do lunch with a prospective employer."

And more and more companies are providing other benefits for their employees: referrals to alcohol rehabilitation programs, on-site child care for working mothers, financial workshops to help older workers prepare for eventual retirement. E.A.P. (Employee Assistance Programs) pay off in a multitude of ways.

It's all part of an overall recognition of the *people side* of quality.

VOLUNTEERS

Employees today not only want to be treated with respect and dignity, but in addition, expect a deeper commitment on the part of the company to recognize the employee is motivated to a great degree by W.I.I.F.M. Peter Drucker, in a speech at Claremont College, spoke of the need for companies to understand that the labor force must be viewed as a group of volunteers who show up to do work for financial remuneration and *for their own reasons.*

People used to work for the basic needs: food and shelter. Then they moved up to working for houses, cars and some of the niceties of life. Then, after World War II, the federal government paid for G.I.'s to go to college. Farmers, plumbers, carpenters—people who might never have aspired to changing occupations—suddenly found themselves exhorted to get a degree and move up in the corporate world. It was both a blessing and a curse for business as well as the workers. Under the corporate rule of the '50's and '60's, families were uprooted every few years to move to new locations under the company umbrella. At dinners and cocktail parties, the primary boast was how many different places they'd lived in since becoming corporate gypsies. It's interesting to me that only resistance from women, who were developing their own careers and refused to be cut off from their opportunities, caused the practice to gradually subside.

During the '70's—sometimes called the Me Decade—the goal was for an accumulation of worldly goods, and the motto was, "The one who dies with the most toys wins." During the '80's, everyone aspired to the luxuries, the hallmarks of having made it: the BMW, the right clothes, the right haircut, the right partner, no matter what the cost in pride or dignity, or the cleat marks left in someone else's back. The Eagles put it best in their song, "Life in the Fast Lane."

Fortunately not all the Baby Boomers are Boesky wannabes; and when jobs are plentiful, the motive of the worker often turns to self-fulfillment. Many of the corporate executives of today were the radicals of the '60's. They were a generation who rebelled against everything, rebelled with their marching, their music, their long hair and their clothes, rebelled with sitting in and sitting out, speaking about peace and brotherhood and love, words that were laughed at and held in contempt in the halls of corporate America. They drove a generation of parents nutty; but they also brought about concern for the environment. Deep in the hearts of many of these flower children, who started out as hippies and turned into yuppies, is still the desire to bring about a better planet through love and breaking down of barriers between people.

A new day is emerging with the W.I.I.F.M. work force. Many of these folks understand working for psychic income, the feeling of pride and the satisfaction of having done a good job, the feeling that you gave something back to the world that day. This is not just doing it right the first time, but doing it for the right *reason* for psychic income.

The managers and leaders of the '90's and beyond, must understand the volunteerism mind-set. When you create a team whose desire is doing right for its own sake, when you experience camaraderie and exceed the expectations of customers, you will have found the key that unlocks the ultimate profit.

INTERVIEW with CAPITAL BANK, Miami, Florida

"We started 18 years ago like a mom and pop shop," says Daniel Holtz, President and Chief Operating Officer. "We knew all the customers by name then. Not only could we recognize them in the street, but we also knew how much they kept on deposit. Things were a lot simpler, then, and the operation ran smoothly. But, as the company grew, performance faltered. We could no longer be that close to the customer. Growth invariably forces you make major changes is the way you do business. You have to develop strong leaders among your employees. Train and empower front line people to do what you used to be able to do yourself. Unfortunately, many people are too late in recognizing the need to make this transition.

"I argued that if we failed to recognize trends and take the necessary steps to correct our course, we risked becoming even more unresponsive. Customers were already leaving us for smaller competitors and employees were never regarded as our most important resource in preventing that."

After a long history of growth, the company gradually became less successful. They began losing one-third of their customer base every year. In a high-volume, low-margin business, customer retention is critical, so Holtz knew that radical changes were necessary for survival. "The customers don't care about your fancy systems and procedures," he says. "To them Capital Bank is the person across the teller window. At the time, I didn't even know it was called quality.

"I called Bob Sherer of Quality Concepts in 1990 and the result was a program to instill quality in every aspect of our business. Nobody can accurately predict corporate America's future, but there's one thing we all know: for any organization to achieve its potential, customer service must be a key business goal. We needed to create a management style more focused on that goal. Improving the quality of customer service was, in my view, a matter of survival.

"The challenge was to keep everything running and increase profitability while at the same time changing the way

we operated. We had to communicate a vision, define what was expected, measure results and reward performance. First and foremost, we had to let employees know we cared about them.

"Training was the key," Holtz says. "Dollars spent in the training area aren't wasted; they'll come back thirty-fold. The first time our managers were told how much we spend on our All Hands Meetings, they nearly fell off their chairs. And now we do it every year, and the price tag goes up because we try to improve on it. But, in 1988 our retail unit was losing money. This year it will make over $5 million, so it pays off. And it's not surprising that our company, as a whole, is producing record earnings, as well. The results come not from doing one thing 100 percent better, but, as Bob says, doing a thousand things 1 percent better."

Since embarking on their quality drive and reorganization, Capital has improved service levels by 78 percent, improved efficiency by $4.8 million and posted healthy annual increases in deposits after three years of flat performance.

"After the quality workshops, the level of customer turnover declined from 29 percent to just under 10 percent over a two-year period, adding nearly $1.7 million to our bottom line. Customers have a much more positive experience with us than they did four years ago. I notice this in the letters I get. I used to get a lot of letters from angry customers; now I get a lot of satisfaction from my correspondence.

"We decided to test a program where we would make ourselves available to customers at any time by appointment. To check on compliance, we had 'mystery' shoppers go to half our offices after hours, and in ten out of 12, the potential customer was invited in and his questions answered.

"About six months later, a director of a competitor, who heard about our quality focus, decided to put us to the test. He called one of our offices and learned it closed at four o'clock, so he deliberately came at 4:30 and knocked on the door. A woman opened it and asked if she could help him. She invited him in, discussed his needs and he ended up opening fourteen accounts, worth over one million dollars."

One of the first innovations at Capital Bank was an All Hands Meeting where everyone was invited to learn more about the company. All employees were given an organizational chart so they'd know where they fit in the company. This was a new idea, because the previous style of management held that if you kept the staff uninformed, you kept them under control. Each employee was asked to fill out an Employee Satisfaction Survey, to tell what was right or wrong about the company. At the next year's meeting, reports showed the progress made in fixing problems, and strengthening what was right. The company gained not only from the basic changes made but through building trust with their employees. Feeling they were treated as equals having important ideas, made people happier at work and, as usual, happy employees translated to happy customers.

One of the questions employees asked was the equivalent of, "How come I'm not making more money?" This was answered by sharing with them how salaries are determined, where capital to grow comes from, and how a strong, growing company means security for their jobs, their raises and their benefits.

They were also told how they could qualify for higher pay by moving into other positions. By understanding the other departments in the company—what they do and how many people are involved—employees could apply for positions in other areas for which they felt qualified. In many cases they went back to school. Tom Flood, executive vice president, says, "We have 45 of our people going to college in the evening, which the bank pays for. It's a wonderful benefit for them which enables them to move forward in the bank and reduces our turnover. When they talk to other people from other companies, they find out that they prefer working for us."

In an early survey, employees asked about their package of benefits; they felt it was inferior to other plans in the marketplace. The result was a change from a mandatory basic benefits package to what is referred to as a "cafeteria" plan, where employees are given a certain amount of credit *each year and can choose whatever benefits they want within the credit limit. Capital even allowed them to take half the credit back if it wasn't spent on benefits. They could have it in cash, or put it in the company's 401K plan, matched 25 percent by the firm. It cost the bank a little more money than the prior year, but employee satisfaction increased dramatically.*

"The needs of a single person are different from those of two people with several children, so it was welcomed by all employees," Holtz says. "Even though it cost us more, the benefits to our employees made it worth the expense. Those kinds of tradeoffs force us every day, as managers, to prove our credibility and our commitment to our employees. Of course, it's all a part of upgrading our cohesiveness and prosperity as a company. It's part of the on-going quality process.

"I tell Bob that I do practically nothing. We've formed quality teams with a cross-section of employees and they're the ones who come up with the good ideas. Very little of my own time is involved. I'm a firm believer that if you ask the right questions of the right people, you get right answers back. By giving our workers the challenge and opportunity to improve the way we do business, they get to the point where they recognize the customer bottlenecks before the customer does. There's no way that management can think of all the quality-related measures the company needs to implement; these things must come from our employees every day. We pay them cash for their good suggestions, and the company has benefited to the tune of over one-half million dollars per year."

"In a quality organization," Tom Flood says, "people will think. The Employee Satisfaction Survey tells us what they think, and we've learned to respond immediately. If an employee sees a need that we should fill, we must do that now; a year from now—even a month—may be too late. As a result, as turnover has decreased, customer service and satisfaction have improved. Customers have told us that if we change personnel, to them it's the same as if they had

changed banks. When they see friendly, familiar faces, they keep coming back; we don't lose them to the competition.

"I believe in strategic actions to meet certain goals. If the strategy doesn't work, change it. Get a new one, but don't change the goal of providing nothing less than total quality."

Daniel Holtz sums it up: "I was committed to making this company profitable every year, every quarter, every month, every job, and I look on the task as exciting because quality is the main ingredient and biggest challenge. From a billion-dollar 'mom and pop shop,' we've become a quality organization of the best people providing excellent service to customers and realizing higher profits."

Challenge: What will you do to train your workers to be the best that they can be for each other, your clients and themselves?

_____

_____

_____

_____

_____

_____

_____

_____

_____

_____

_____

_____

_____

THE RIGHT THING

The so-called new morality is too often the old immorality condoned.

Lord Shawcross

SHAMROCK REAL ESTATE

I found the meaning of the "Ultimate Profit" one night when I attended a Girl Scout meeting—the first with my daughter—where I met Rich Reis. He was a good Portuguese boy, and had no education beyond a high school diploma. His parents had nothing, his dad was an alcoholic, and Rich worked for everything he had. He drove a truck delivering non-food items to grocery stores, got married, had three kids and a little house. I was leading salesman of the year for my corporation and I told him, "You've got to get into sales." I took him in for an interview, but he didn't join; instead he went into real estate. He went to school at night to learn and then started to work at it on weekends. Finally he quit his driving job, bought a couple of little houses for $20,000 and he and his wife worked painting them inside and out and then rented them. Soon he had a large number of rental properties and his own real estate company. Today his net worth is over $7 million.

Rich never screwed anyone in his life. In the early days, he walked away from deals that would have made him rich a lot faster but weren't ethical. People laughed at him, but no one ever got the best of him and he can live with his conscience.

A mutual friend once asked him if he had trouble with tenants in his rental properties. He said, "No, if I treat them right, they treat me right. I paint the outside every five years. I fix things when they break. People don't destroy my property because they know I don't raise the rent arbitrarily. I look at the property regularly. If someone sprays graffiti on a building I own, I have it painted out within the hour."

What a simple, old-fashioned system. But it works.

ENTREPRENEURS / INTRAPRENEURS

There are many more stories that could be told, but they're still a small percentage. For over 30 years now I've watched as some business people achieved a certain position in a company and then felt the lack of challenge in their day-to-day responsibility. These are the people who look for an opportunity to break free of their current work life. They go to entrepreneurial fairs where franchisers of yogurt shops, quick print companies, dry cleaners, etc., show their wares.

When my wife was selling her business some years ago, she had many prospective buyers talk to her endlessly about the cash flow, the employees, the customers, and the equipment. They bubbled over with enthusiasm at the possibility of being their own boss, filled with excitement and optimism. Then, just as suddenly they disappeared and she never heard from them again.

It reminded me of the many times I heard employees grouse about their jobs, but when pressed for reasons why they didn't jump ship, made excuses such as loyalty or not wanting to leave a company in the lurch during bad times. The truth was they were afraid of the unknown, of going through the interview process to get another job and starting all over again to create relationships and find out where the bodies are buried in the next company. They wanted to become entrepreneurs, but stark terror at the thought of leaving regular pay checks, medical plans, company cars, and private secretaries quickly reduced their plans to mere daydreams; and it would take a Scud missile to dislodge them from their multi-benefitted environment.

Some managers, who are disenchanted with the humdrum work day, turn to sports to fill the void. They know all the teams, have favorites, and wear their jackets, their hats, their shirts, know every statistic. Being a fan is fun, but some people carry these activities to extremes; they become sports freaks. You'd almost think that the team is paying them for their support because it has become such an obsession.

It's not unhealthy to have an interest in your home team, or the local playhouse or your church choir. In fact, it's commendable to work for your community in your leisure time. It helps to clear the mind and cleanse the soul. But if we're so dissatisfied with the job that pays our wages, that we go to extremes to blot it from our consciousness, or toy with the idea of buying a franchise—anything at all—just to get away from it, we should be examining our priorities more closely.

It's very difficult for some people to get out of their comfort zone. The ruts are so deep, they've even decorated them. It's like trying to get them out of the way of an oncoming train. They see it, hear it, smell it, but will risk death rather than change to the unknown, which will usually turn out to be better.

I offer a challenge to executives and managers: if you honestly don't intend to quit that job, or retire early, why not become an intrapreneur? That is, become an entrepreneur right where you are? Start your own effort for improvement within your organization. Challenge yourself and your people and you'll get your blood flowing and find that excitement can exist wherever you choose to make it. Instead of rooting for a sports team, build your own team of workers, motivate them, provide some goals and rewards, establish your own Super Bowl of excellence and find job satisfaction that not only inspires your day but pays off on the bottom line.

Anybody who's been thinking seriously about quality for more than a few minutes knows you don't change quality in a program. It's a process. Faced with a need for improvement, some managers take a very sharp razor and cut right down to the bone, which can be destructive. You can't achieve excellence in a hurry. You need to get everyone into the boat and find out which oar to pull and go in the same direction.

If your company is losing $10 million a month, it's hard to wait, to move the dial slowly. How long can you do that until your company is dead? How do you save the patient and impart quality at the same time? I don't believe you have to cut it to the bone before you can begin to enhance performance. There are a lot of ways to cut: the executive perks, the golden parachutes, making a company profitable on paper while killing the patient. A buggy whip factory has to go under, but if the company has built a championship team, it can be saved with new products and services.

If it's a large organization, break it up into six or seven different units and let the people who are already responsible for those units run it, a bottoms up approach. Frequently, if they have the authority, they can turn their units around. A recent article in *Fortune* Magazine told of a raider who came into a large company and sold off some divisions to the people who were running those divisions. They became very successful, because they didn't have to feed the corporate monster.

You must believe in your heart that employees are your most valuable asset. They're already on the payroll; you don't have to hire an outsider. Unfortunately, most employees don't get opportunities to show what they can do. Some don't even know the people at the top. In the film, *Roger and Me*, Roger Smith of General Motors wouldn't even let Michael Moore in to see him.

I sat in a corporate meeting a few years ago and the CEO didn't even know exactly where the company's production facilities were located. He flew in from California to run the company from its headquarters Monday to Friday. It had to do with finances, big cigars and motor cars; it had little to do with employees or customers, or building a climate for success.

Greed and low quality of life isn't exclusive to business. It's rampant in the government sector. Politicians take trips to fancy resorts at the expense of the taxpayer. Some policemen start out doing the right thing and end up taking bribes. Look at the savings and loan scandal. You can't have people looking at that and not begin to think that everyone else is doing it so why not me? A good person makes everybody else look bad, so they soon get rid of the honest ones. We have to protect and encourage the whistle-blowers if we want quality in government and industry.

When high school students will kill one another for a leather jacket or a pair of Reeboks, we have a real problem. I'm reminded of the character of Alex Keaton on *Family Ties*. In that television show he was extremely right-wing, while his parents were flower children of the '60's. It was funny back in the '80's, because we had all begun to believe the ends justified the means. But, when 13-year-olds are hijacking cars at gunpoint, when a generation of kids runs through the streets with automatic weapons in their hands, it's not funny any more. In the United States today as many people die of gunshot wounds in a single day as do in Japan in an entire year. New York averages 200 robberies a day, Tokyo two. It's clear to me that the Japanese are teaching their young people a whole lot more than higher mathematics and how to do quality work on an assembly line!

Where are the heroes and role models for our people today? Do the kids say, "When I get big I want to be like Marion Barry" (The former mayor of Washington, D.C. who went to jail for drug possession)? Then there's Donald Trump. Just a few years ago everything he did was golden. He was bigger than life, someone to emulate. But he started out with a $20 million gift from his father and has since leveraged everything he owns. He has power over billions of dollars, but if those loans should be called, he won't have enough cash to cover them. He has *less* than no money! Is that a lesson we want to teach our kids?

Unfortunately, it seems the biggest motivator we have in our society today is greed. Through television advertising we teach our children to want things. They think they have to have everything they see. Then they go to school and cheat on their tests. They don't care how they get the $70,000 a year and the Lexus. *Things* are their motivators. "I have to buy things from fancy stores because what my neighbor thinks about me is more important than what *I* think about me." There are women in wealthy neighborhoods who go to bars and sell their bodies so they can buy expensive shoes. Is that a sad commentary?

RIGHT REASONS

The ultimate product is not flying first class. If you do things for the right reasons you will get some of life's perks. The bread you cast on the water *will* come back to you, but that can't be the reason you do it.

If you look at the list of people trying to bring real quality improvement to their work, those at the top are performance fanatics. Their companies can win the Malcolm Baldrige Award. They walk it, they talk it. They live it. You can sense it in them.

The people at the bottom of the list are only interested in current profits. I call it the short-term MBA mentality. Too many American business people care only about the next quarter. They look at the next promotion, or wait for retirement. They aren't going to make any changes and that's that.

In between them and the performance fanatics, there's another group I call Latent Performance Fanatics. I believe that this group is expanding, because quality is tied into long term profitability. It's not a quarter-to-quarter issue. Latent P.F.'s are the people who would really like to offer quality service and live a quality life but are struggling with how to do it.

Since leaving the corporate jungle, I try to reach that group, to be a catalyst, a quality advocate, someone who can help them, give them strength and support, light the way.

P.F.'s are special and scarce and in great demand. The rest read the articles, and some are beginning to focus on quality because they're seeing that it affects the bottom line. I say, there's a better reason for doing it. Do it the right way the first time and for *the right reasons*.

I think many people don't know why they should be working on quality. They say, "everybody's doing it, so we'd better do it too." Or because it sounds good. The real reason to practice quality is because it makes sense to you. One of the things that drove me to start Quality Concepts was the fact that some companies I saw up close and personal had a program because they were *supposed* to. They threw some money at it and said, "Now we have a quality program. Lets go on to something else." They didn't understand the root cause of excellence.

Quality is a way of life, not just good business. True quality and long term growth mean doing it for the right reasons, not for the bottom line or to get the plaque on the wall. The real reason to do it is because—like Wilford Brimley says about oatmeal—"it's the right thing to do." It should be our mission, no matter what we do: running Boys Town or running the Police Athletic League or the mom and pop store.

Once again, quality is not a program; it's a process. But, more important, it's a process of life. It's personal development, it's life oriented. The ultimate profit is the time that you have and the way that you spend it, because time is a gift. Do you use your time to write poetry, books or sermons, or to scrawl graffiti on fences? To spare human pain, or to torture others to get what you want? Quality is a value, not just a sound business practice.

In *Passions and Prejudices* (McGraw-Hill), Leo Rosten says, "I cannot believe that the purpose of life is to be 'happy.' I think the purpose of life is to be useful, to be responsible, to be compassionate. It is, above all, to matter, to count, to stand for something, to have made some difference that you lived at all."

We're the only animal on the face of the earth with the gift of logic. A cow can't do logical thinking or decision making. Think about that in your personal life and your work. You will spend more waking time at work than you do with your family. Isn't it logical to spend that time with good people, doing a quality job? Then, when you get to the end of your life you can say, "I did some good stuff." That's the real bottom line, *the ultimate profit.*

During my Performance Plus Leadership Workshops, I ask, "How many of you have ever spent even half a day thinking about how you make decisions?" Rarely does anyone raise a hand. Most people don't think they have control over their lives. Some are stuck in jobs that they dislike or tolerate. I trace it back to ignorance, greed or fear. Remember that, of Dr. Deming's 14 Points, number eight was fear. When you made a decision, did you make it out of fear or ignorance? Did you simply do what someone else told you? Or was it, "How do I get my $70,000 and Lexus?" That's the greed, the Boesky effect. In the movie *Wall Street*, the characters made decisions based on what material things they could acquire, epitomized in Gordon Gecko's statement, "Greed is good."

I've always been in favor of military or other mandatory service, which is required in many countries. It's not necessarily going to war. If people go into the service of mankind for a couple of years—help the elderly or disabled, or go into a Peace Corps-like program and build houses for the poor as do Capital Bank and HomeBanc—perhaps more of them will find they get their lights turned on. Our whole society needs some adjusting, and quality is a part of that. All society needs a redirection in values, turning from greed to acknowledge the fact that we're in a global society now, a gigantic glass bowl. We can't make a lot of money by forever snowing others. The big picture is forcing us to grow up and change.

I'm not a flaming liberal, worried about the screw-ees of the world. I'm talking about the people who have been screwers all their lives and suddenly realize that was a sad way to spend their time. How do they feel about themselves? Did they earn any psychic income?

If your financial portfolio makes you feel good, that's okay. If you go to the company picnic and enjoy being there, that's okay too. The money is a come-along; you can't keep it from you when you do the right thing for the right reasons. Real psychic income is a very different thing. It's recognizing the necessity of quality in what you do with your limited time on earth. You could call it selfishness, but it's not the same as greed. Rather, it's the habit of ennobling the "self."

That's what working should really be about; it should be the best time of your life. There's one particular time that I remember, and it wasn't when I made the most money. It was when I worked with a group of people that I really loved and cared about. I couldn't wait to get to work every day. It was James M. Barrie who said, "Those who bring sunlight into the lives of others cannot keep it from themselves."

We need to click the dial a centimeter toward excellence every day, and we each should say, "I'm doing it for me because I want to help others. It's highly personal and when I get through with it I'm going to feel good about me." Oh, and, yes, incidentally, it's good for the bottom line.

At the risk of sounding like a moralist, I think the ultimate profit is the joy of spending your life doing things that make you proud, the right things. Peter Drucker spoke a profound truth when he said: "Ethics stays in the prefaces of the average business science book." In my early years, I did some things wrong. When I woke up, I started doing the right things for the right reasons. I still make dumb mistakes, but I admit it, learn and move on. I've tried to take ethics out of the preface and put it where we can look at it more often, and try to practice it every day, one day at a time.

My years with Quality Concepts have shown me conclusively that quality practices can be taught to executives, managers, and employees. Furthermore, that this process not only improves the product or service provided by American businesses, but also the morale of everyone involved, and—equally important—adds growth to the economy.

I'm not saying that only by hiring Quality Concepts can you achieve these results. What I am saying is that unless these ideas are put into practice in more American businesses, we will continue to lose ground, not only to the Japanese, but to all the Asian rim, to the unified Germany and to the newly emerging eastern European countries. We have no time to waste. We need to Do the Right Thing, for the Right Reasons and Right Now!

Challenge: What will you do to promote ethics in your organization and in your life?

_____

_____

_____

_____

_____

_____

Let us know how your challenges work out!

Quality Concepts
2659 Townsgate Road
Suite 215
Westlake Village, CA 91361
1-800-545-3998

To order copies of this book or our audio tape set *Quality Means Survival and Nothing Less* at $29.95, please see the order form at the back of this book—or call us at the number shown above.

As a bonus for ordering, you will receive a full four-issue subscription to our newsletter *Communicating for Services.*

RECOMMENDED READING

On Becoming a Leader, by Warren Bennis, Addison-Wesley Publication, 1989.

Dynamic Decision Maker, by Kenneth Brousseau and Philip Hunsake, Harper & Row, 1990.

The Machine That Changed the World, M.I.T., Womack-Rawson Assoc., 1990

American Business: A Two-Minute Warning, By C. Jackson Grayson Jr. & Carla O'Dell, The Free Press, 1988.

Barbarians to Bureaucrats, by Lawrence M. Miller, Faucett Columbine, 1990

The Goal, by Eliyahu M. Godratt, North River Press, 1986.

Teaching the Elephant to Dance, by James A. Belasco, Plume, 1991

The Customer Comes Second, by Hal Rosenbluth, Morrow, 1992.

The Fifth Discipline Field Book, by Peter Senge, Art Kleiner, Charlotte Roberts, Richard Ross and Bryan Smith, Currency Doubleday, 1994.

INDEX

ILLUSTRATIONS

Order Form

- ⬛ **Fax orders**: 1-805-496-5841

- ☎ **Telephone orders**: Call toll free 1-800-545-3998. Have your VISA or MasterCard ready.

- ✉ **Postal orders**: Performance Plus, 2659 Townsgate Rd. Suite 215, Westlake Village, CA 91361

Please send the following:

Books:	Qty		Total
Doing the Right Thing:	_____	@ $29.95	_____
Fear and the Bottom Line:	_____	@ $29.95	_____
Audio Cassette Tape Set:			
Quality Means Survival	_____	@ $29.95	_____
(A four-tape audio set)			
	Grand total before tax		_____

Company name:_____

Name:_____

Address:_____

City:_____State:_____Zip:_____

Telephone: (_____)_____

Sales tax:
Please add 7.75% for books shipped to California addresses.

Shipping:
First Class: $4.50 per item. Call for orders of 10 or more items.
Fed Ex: Call for overnight shipping rates.

Payment:
❑   Check
❑   Credit Card: ❑VISA,   ❑MasterCard

Card Number:_____

Name on card:_____Exp. date:_____

Quantity discounts may apply. Call for information.